Juicing for Beginners

The Ultimate Guide to Dropping Pounds & Boosting Energy in 30 Days!

By Seraphina Forest

Table Of Content

Introduction

The Transformative Power of Juicing

At the intersection of tradition and innovation, juicing stands as a testament to our innate desire for health and vitality. For centuries, civilizations around the world have recognized the profound benefits hidden within the fruits and vegetables that the Earth generously offers. Juicing, in its essence, is about unlocking these benefits in a concentrated, flavorful form. It represents a journey of discovery, a harmonious dance between nature's bounty and human ingenuity.

While many of us have enjoyed a fresh glass of orange juice or savored the vibrant colors of a mixed fruit smoothie, the world of juicing stretches far beyond these simple delights. It's not just about taste or refreshment. Juicing has the transformative power to rejuvenate, heal, and invigorate. Every drop extracted is a potent blend of nutrients, antioxidants, and enzymes, each with its unique role in nurturing our body.

Yet, what truly makes juicing transformative is its ability to be both a mirror and a window. As a mirror, it reflects our personal health choices, desires, and aspirations. Each juice we craft can be tailored to our unique needs, whether it's a boost of energy, a calming tonic, or a nutritional powerhouse. As a window, juicing offers a glimpse into the vast world of natural wellness, opening doors to new flavors, traditions, and knowledge.

In recent years, the rising wave of health consciousness has brought juicing to the forefront, not just as a trend but as a lifestyle. As our lives grow increasingly complex, the allure of simplicity becomes undeniable. Juicing is that bridge to simplicity, a way to connect with the primal act of nourishing our bodies and souls with nature's purest offerings.

Setting Expectations: What This Book Will Achieve

We stand at the doorway of an enlightening journey, one that weaves through the intricate landscapes of health, wellness, and the art of juicing. However, before we tread forward, it's pivotal to understand the path we're about to embark on and set clear expectations for this odyssey.

The realm of juicing is vast, brimming with potential, but often shrouded in misconceptions, half-truths, and overwhelming amounts of information. This book is your compass, designed to navigate these waters with clarity, offering direction, and shedding light on the true essence of juicing. It's not just a guide, but a commitment to authenticity, a promise to provide genuine insights backed by research, experience, and a deep respect for nature's wisdom.

One of the primary objectives is to demystify juicing. While the process might seem straightforward—extracting juice from fruits and vegetables—the underlying science, the choices of ingredients, the techniques, and the profound impact on our health, make juicing an art form in its own right. This book will delve deep into these facets, ensuring you not only grasp the 'how' but also understand the 'why'.

More than just recipes and techniques, this book aims to instill a mindset. Juicing, at its core, is a philosophy. It's about making conscious choices for one's health, about respecting the intricate balance of nature, and about celebrating the joys of vitality. This holistic perspective will be a recurring theme throughout, offering readers a comprehensive view of juicing as both a practice and a lifestyle.

Lastly, this journey is meant to be empowering. Whether you're a seasoned juicing enthusiast or someone taking their first tentative steps, this book aims to equip you with knowledge, inspire creativity, and ignite a passion for natural wellness. As we turn each page, it's my hope that you'll not only discover the wonders of juicing but also embrace its transformative potential in your life. Let's set the stage, align our expectations, and delve into the vibrant world of juicing with enthusiasm and curiosity.

Chapter 1: Foundations of Juicing

History of Juicing: A Brief Overview

The ritual of consuming liquids to nourish the body isn't a trend that emerged a decade ago, nor even a century ago. The history of juicing stretches back thousands of years, with its roots deeply intertwined with the story of civilization itself. While today's bustling streets see urban dwellers clutching bottles of green elixirs, this is but a new chapter in the age-old narrative of juicing.

In ancient civilizations, medicinal practitioners would squeeze out the juices of specific plants and fruits, believing in their therapeutic qualities. They discerned the power hidden within the liquid essence of nature. Ancient Greeks, known for their profound wisdom and holistic approaches, often referred to the 'nectar of the gods', hinting at a liquid that provides vigor, strength, and vitality. While the exact recipe remains shrouded in myth, it's plausible that the Greeks were onto some form of early juicing, appreciating the condensed nutrition and vitality that came from the essence of nature.

Journeying East: The Age-Old Tradition

As we journey eastward in our historical expedition, ancient Chinese traditions revered certain juices for their medicinal qualities. Traditional Chinese Medicine (TCM) has, for eons, recommended the liquid from specific berries, roots, and herbs as remedies for ailments ranging from the common cold to more chronic conditions. And, not to be forgotten, there's Ayurveda, an ancient Indian healing system that recognized the potent benefits of specific juices. Turmeric, ginger, and certain leafy greens were often recommended in liquid form to balance the body's doshas or energies, pointing to an understanding of the concentrated power of nature's produce.

The Western Evolution

Fast forward to the last couple of centuries, and we see a noticeable shift in the Western world's approach to juicing. The 20th century, with its technological advancements, brought forth electric juicers and blenders, allowing for more households to explore juicing's benefits beyond a luxury. Dr. Norman Walker, in the 1930s, was a pioneer in promoting the health benefits of fresh vegetable juices. His work emphasized not just the nutritional richness of juices, but also their potential to detoxify the body.

It's essential to understand that while juicing's popularity might seem like a modern-day phenomenon, especially with the rise of health cafes and juice bars, it's an age-old practice. What has changed, however, is our understanding of nutrition, the vast variety of ingredients we now have access to, and our innovative methods of extraction.

By looking at this rich tapestry of history, we gain respect for juicing as not just a trend, but a time-tested method of nourishing our bodies. It's a blend of ancient wisdom and modern science, a bridge connecting our past's natural practices with today's health-conscious lifestyles. Through this book, we aim to explore this bridge further, ensuring that the juice you pour into your glass is not just a drink, but a legacy of health.

The Science Behind Juicing: Nutritional Breakdown

At its core, juicing is a process of extracting the liquid content from fruits and vegetables. But what is it about this liquid that has garnered attention across millennia? The answer lies in the unique concentration of nutrients, phytochemicals, and enzymes present in the juice.

A Symphony of Nutrients
When you bite into an apple or munch on a carrot, you're enjoying a mix of fibers, water, vitamins, and minerals. While the act of chewing and digesting is beneficial, the process of juicing breaks down the cellular walls of these fruits and vegetables, making the nutrients more immediately accessible to your body.

Vitamins like C, A, E, and several of the B-complex family are abundant in many fruits and vegetables. These are water-soluble, meaning they can be easily extracted during the juicing process and quickly absorbed by our digestive systems. Minerals like potassium, magnesium, and calcium also find their way into the juice, providing a myriad of health benefits from maintaining heart rhythm to ensuring bone health.

Phytochemical Powerhouses
Beyond vitamins and minerals, fruits and vegetables are home to thousands of phytochemicals – compounds produced by plants that often have health-promoting properties. Lycopene in tomatoes, flavonoids in citrus fruits, and glucosinolates in cruciferous vegetables are just a few examples. The juicing process amplifies the concentration of these compounds, turning your glass of juice into a phytochemical powerhouse. While research on these compounds continues to evolve, many are linked to anti-inflammatory, anti-oxidant, and even anti-cancer properties.

Enzymatic Excellence
Enzymes are the catalysts for countless metabolic processes in our bodies. Freshly extracted juices are rich in natural enzymes that can enhance digestion and absorption. When fruits and vegetables are juiced, especially at cold temperatures, these enzymes remain active, ensuring that your body gets a burst of enzymatic activity with every sip.

A Note on Fiber
One of the often-raised points about juicing is the reduction of dietary fiber since the extraction process leaves behind the pulp. While fiber is essential for digestive health and maintaining steady blood sugar levels, juicing doesn't have to replace whole fruit and vegetable consumption entirely. Think of juicing as a supplement to your diet – a way to increase your nutrient intake without necessarily increasing calorie intake significantly.

Differentiating Juicing from Other Dietary Trends

In our modern world, where new dietary trends emerge seemingly overnight, it's crucial to understand where juicing fits in. Unlike many diets that ebb and flow with fashion, juicing has deep historical roots. But what sets it apart from the myriad of other food and drink practices? Let's demystify juicing in the context of other popular dietary trends.

Juicing vs. Smoothies
At first glance, juicing and making smoothies might appear identical—after all, both involve turning fruits and vegetables into a drinkable form. However, while juicing extracts the liquid and leaves the pulp behind, smoothies blend the entire fruit or vegetable, including its fiber. The blending process creates a thicker consistency and retains more of the whole food's properties. Juicing offers a more concentrated nutrient intake, while smoothies provide a fuller, more satiating experience due to the fiber content.

Juicing and Detox Diets
Detox diets often promise rapid weight loss and body cleansing by following a restrictive diet, sometimes emphasizing juices. While juicing can be a component of these regimens, it's essential to differentiate between a juice-focused diet and a balanced approach to juicing. This book's philosophy emphasizes integrating juicing into a balanced lifestyle rather than using it as a short-term, extreme solution.

Comparing with Fad Diets

From high-protein diets to those cutting out specific food groups, fad diets often come with big promises. While some people might experience short-term benefits, these diets aren't always sustainable or balanced. Juicing, in contrast, is more of a practice than a diet. It complements your existing eating habits, enhancing nutrient intake rather than restricting or eliminating foods.

Juicing as a Supplement, Not a Replacement

One of the key distinctions between juicing and many dietary trends is its intention. Juicing is not about replacing meals or essential food groups. Instead, it's about supplementing and enriching your current diet. A glass of fresh juice should be viewed as a nutrient-packed addition to your daily intake, not as a complete meal replacement.

Chapter 2: Equipment & Tools

Types of Juicers: Centrifugal vs. Masticating vs. Triturating

Venturing into the world of juicing, one of the first and most pivotal decisions you'll encounter is choosing the right type of juicer. It's akin to an artist selecting their preferred brush; each choice brings its unique touch, influencing the end result. While the ultimate objective remains the same—extracting juice—understanding the nuances between the different types of juicers is crucial for achieving the best results tailored to your needs.

Centrifugal Juicers: The Speedy Maestros

Imagine the refreshing gust of wind you feel from a swiftly spinning fan on a hot summer's day. Centrifugal juicers employ a similar mechanism. Equipped with a rapidly rotating blade, these juicers chop up fruits and vegetables at impressive speeds, extracting the juice via the force of centrifugation. Their prowess lies in their speed. If you're someone constantly on-the-go, looking for a quick glass of vitality before dashing out the door, a centrifugal juicer might just be your trusty ally. However, this rapid action often means a bit more heat and oxidation, which can influence the juice's nutrient profile and shelf life.

Masticating Juicers: The Thoughtful Artisans

Taking the road less traveled, masticating juicers are the antithesis of haste. These machines, often referred to as "cold-press" juicers, function by crushing and pressing the ingredients. The result? A methodical extraction that champions nutrient retention and delivers a richer, fuller taste. The leisurely pace may require a bit more patience, but the reward is a glass brimming with nature's essence, often with less froth and a longer shelf life.

Triturating Juicers: The Connoisseurs of Perfection

Enter the realm of precision with triturating juicers. Operating with twin gears that rotate inwards, these juicers are the epitome of thoroughness. They extract juice by grinding ingredients between their powerful gears, ensuring even the most fibrous greens surrender their liquid treasure. While they do come with a heftier price tag, the investment is evident in the unparalleled juice quality—dense, vibrant, and bursting with flavor.

A Deep Dive: Deciphering Your Juicing Needs

Each type of juicer shines in its own light, and understanding your personal needs and priorities can guide you towards making the best choice.

Noise Level and Kitchen Real Estate
Centrifugal juicers tend to be the noisiest of the trio. Their high-speed rotation can create a din comparable to a blender. If you're an early riser, this might disrupt a peaceful morning. Masticating and triturating juicers, on the other hand, hum along at lower decibels, making them more neighbor-friendly.

In terms of size, centrifugal juicers generally have a larger footprint, necessitating more counter space. Conversely, masticating juicers, with their vertical design, might snugly fit into tighter kitchen spaces, while triturating juicers, with their elongated form, require a bit more horizontal real estate.

Versatility: Beyond Just Juicing
While all three types are champions in juice extraction, if you're seeking versatility, masticating and triturating juicers take the lead. Many of these machines come with attachments that allow for other kitchen tasks such as making nut butters, grinding coffee, or even extruding pasta. Centrifugal juicers, being specialized in their craft, typically don't offer these additional functionalities.

Economic Considerations: Initial and Long-Term Investment
Upfront costs can vary significantly. Centrifugal juicers tend to be the most wallet-friendly, making them an appealing choice for beginners. Masticating juicers sit in the mid-range, while triturating juicers often carry a premium price, reflecting their superior juice yield and quality.

However, when contemplating cost, it's wise to consider long-term investment. While you might save initially with a centrifugal juicer, their slightly lower juice yield means potentially buying more produce in the long run. Masticating and triturating juicers, with their impressive extraction rates, might balance out the initial costs over time with savings on ingredients.

Embarking on a Juicing Adventure: Essential Tools for Success

Every art form has its tools, and juicing is no different. Venturing into the realm of juicing can seem like an intimidating endeavor, but it becomes a joyous experience with the right equipment. Beyond the juicer itself, there are several tools that can greatly enhance your juicing journey.

A Trustworthy Cutting Board and Knife

Before anything goes into your juicer, it has to be prepared. A durable, non-slip cutting board provides a secure platform for chopping fruits and vegetables. Couple that with a sharp chef's knife, and you'll reduce prep time, ensuring that your produce is cut cleanly and efficiently. Remember, the better you treat your ingredients before they reach the juicer, the higher quality juice you'll receive in return.

Citrus Reamer or Hand Press

While many juicers can handle citrus fruits, sometimes you want just a touch of tanginess without the hassle of setting up your main machine. In these cases, a simple citrus reamer or hand press becomes invaluable.
Whether you're looking to add a splash of lemon to your green juice or craft a fresh orange blend, these tools are perfect for quick citrus juicing.

Fine Mesh Strainer

For those who prefer a smoother juice, a fine mesh strainer can be a game-changer. By pouring your juice through one, you can filter out any remaining pulp or foam. The result? A silky, velvety beverage that glides down effortlessly, ensuring you savor every drop.

Glass Storage Bottles

Investing in high-quality glass storage bottles will keep your juices fresh and vibrant. Unlike plastic, which can sometimes impart an unwanted taste or leach chemicals, glass preserves the purity of your juice. With airtight lids, these bottles can maintain freshness, allowing you to enjoy your concoctions even a day or two after juicing.

Flexible Measuring Spoons and Cups

While juicing is often about experimentation and personal taste, sometimes precision is needed, especially when following specific recipes or when you're trying to maintain consistent flavor profiles.

Flexible measuring tools make it simple to pour and measure liquids, ensuring that every juice you craft has just the right balance.

Chapter 3: Ingredients 101

The Symphony of Fruits: An Ode to Vibrant Health and Flavor

Imagine, for a moment, standing in an orchard bathed in the soft glow of the morning sun. Rows of apple trees stretch as far as the eye can see, their branches weighed down by gleaming, dew-kissed fruit. Nearby, berry bushes burst with color, and citrus trees emanate an invigorating aroma. This scene is not just a picturesque landscape; it is nature's pharmacy, where each fruit holds secrets to our well-being.

The Melodious Apple: Nature's Vitamin Powerhouse

Take the apple, for instance. Often hailed as an everyday snack, the apple is much more than a quick bite. Rich in dietary fiber, particularly pectin, apples are allies for our digestive system. Their subtle sweetness is accompanied by a range of vitamins and minerals, with vitamin C leading the charge. But it's not just about vitamins; the magic lies in the polyphenols—compounds that have been researched for their potential antioxidant properties.

Berries: Nature's Jewels of Antioxidants

Then come the berries: blueberries, strawberries, raspberries, and their kin. These small fruits pack a punch well above their weight. Bursting with flavor, they also boast a nutritional profile that reads like a who's who of antioxidants. Anthocyanins, the compounds that give berries their vivid colors, have become a focal point for studies on cognitive health and aging.

Citrus Chronicles: Zesty Tales of Vitamin C

The world of citrus—lemons, oranges, grapefruits—is an invigorating realm of zest and zeal. Beyond their vibrant flavors, they are champions of vitamin C, a nutrient known for its role in immune system function.
But that's not all. Citrus fruits are also abundant in flavonoids, which are being researched for their potential cardiovascular benefits.

The Kaleidoscope of Use

Every fruit has its story, its unique profile of nutrients, and its ideal use in juicing. While apples provide a balanced sweetness, making them versatile for various juice blends, the tartness of berries can uplift and invigorate a morning drink. Citrus fruits, with their zest, can transform a simple juice into a refreshing elixir of health.

Venturing Beyond the Green: The Colorful Landscape of Vegetables

When one thinks of juicing, the immediate image is often a vivid shade of green. This is no surprise, as green juices, often composed of leafy vegetables like spinach, kale, and chard, have taken the spotlight in recent years. But to dwell only in the verdant realm is to miss the diverse spectrum of nutrition and taste that other vegetables offer.

Beneath the soil's surface, a world of nutrient-rich roots thrives, waiting to be tapped. Carrots, with their sweet undertones and vibrant orange hue, are not only a visual treat but a treasure trove of beta-carotene, a precursor to vitamin A. And then there's the beetroot, with its deep crimson color, an indication of its rich stores of nitrates and antioxidants. These nitrates are converted into nitric oxide in the body, a compound that has been associated with improved blood flow and lower blood pressure.

The Unassuming Power of Cruciferous Vegetables
Broccoli, cauliflower, and Brussels sprouts, while perhaps not the darlings of the dinner table during our childhood, have grown into nutritional superheroes in the world of wellness.
Rich in compounds like sulforaphane, which has been researched for its potential cancer-fighting properties, these vegetables are a testament to the idea that sometimes, power comes from unexpected sources.

Peppers and Tomatoes: The Sunlit Delights
Venture further, and you'll discover the sun-loving vegetables like bell peppers and tomatoes. Lycopene, the compound that gifts tomatoes their signature red hue, has garnered attention for its potential antioxidant properties. On the other hand, bell peppers, especially the red ones, are vitamin C champions, often surpassing even the citrus fruits in concentration.

Diverse Yet Harmonious
Each vegetable, whether it thrives beneath the earth, basks in the sun, or stands tall and leafy, contributes uniquely to the juicing experience. The sweet embrace of a carrot, the potent depths of broccoli, or the zesty kiss of a bell pepper all enrich our palates, offering layers of flavors and nutrients.

Herbs and Spices: Elixirs of Flavor and Wellness

In the world of juicing, fruits and vegetables often dominate the conversation. Yet, nestled in the corners of our kitchens and gardens, herbs and spices silently hold their ground, packed with flavors and therapeutic qualities that can elevate our juicing experience from the ordinary to the sublime.

The Herbal Alchemists

Consider basil, an aromatic delight that's not just for your Italian dishes. This fragrant herb, when juiced, not only adds a refreshing twist but is also known for its anti-inflammatory and anti-bacterial properties.

Mint, another common kitchen resident, offers a cool reprieve, especially during warmer months. Its soothing effects on the digestive system have been celebrated in culinary and medicinal circles for ages.

Cilantro, often polarizing in the culinary world for its distinct taste, is a detoxifying powerhouse in juices. Rich in antioxidants, it has been said to help with the removal of heavy metals from our bodies, ensuring our system functions smoothly.

The Spice Trail

Spices, often reserved for hot dishes, have found a unique place in the realm of cold juices. Take turmeric, for example. This golden-hued root, a staple in Indian cuisine, contains curcumin, which has anti-inflammatory and antioxidant properties. A dash of freshly juiced turmeric can not only add a warm, earthy flavor but also provides a myriad of health benefits.

Ginger, with its zesty and spicy undertones, can awaken even the most mundane of juices. Beyond its taste, ginger is renowned for its anti-inflammatory properties and its ability to soothe digestive woes. Just a small chunk can elevate a juice, offering warmth and depth.

Synergistic Blends

It's the combination of these herbs and spices with fruits and vegetables that creates a symphony of flavors and health benefits. Imagine the tanginess of pineapple paired with the warmth of ginger or the sweetness of apple dancing with the coolness of mint. These blends not only tantalize our taste buds but ensure that with each sip, we're nourishing our bodies holistically.

The Importance of Organic Ingredients: Beyond the Label

The journey of juicing is as much about the quality of ingredients as it is about flavor combinations and nutrition. As we delve into the world of fresh produce, a question inevitably arises: Why should one opt for organic ingredients? What makes them stand apart in this vast sea of readily available fruits, vegetables, herbs, and spices?

Nature in its Purest Form

Organic produce harkens back to the traditional ways of farming – where the earth was revered, and agriculture was more than just a business. It was an intimate dance between man and nature. Organic farming steers clear of synthetic pesticides, herbicides, and genetically modified organisms (GMOs). The result? Ingredients that are as close to their natural state as possible, bearing the true essence of the soil they came from.

The Nutritional Edge

While the taste of organic produce often speaks for itself, the benefits run deeper. Several studies suggest that organic fruits and vegetables might contain higher levels of certain vitamins, minerals, and antioxidants compared to their conventionally grown counterparts. For instance, the rich, vibrant colors in organic berries or the deep greens in spinach are not just pleasing to the eye; they are indicative of the dense nutrients packed within.

Safety and Sustainability

Choosing organic is also a step towards consuming produce that's free from potentially harmful synthetic chemicals. Over time, the residue from these chemicals might accumulate in our bodies, raising concerns about long-term health effects.

Furthermore, organic farming practices prioritize sustainability. By maintaining soil health, reducing pollution, and conserving water, these methods ensure that the land remains fertile and productive for future generations. It's a holistic approach that views the farm as a living entity, where every element, from the tiniest microorganism in the soil to the humans tending to the crops, plays a crucial role.

Chapter 4: The Art & Science of Recipe Creation

Balancing Taste and Nutrition

The key is to find that sweet spot, where taste and health dance together in a harmonious waltz. For instance, the slight bitterness of greens can be offset by the natural sweetness of carrots or apples, without overpowering the drink with sugar. Likewise, the tanginess of citrus fruits, like oranges or lemons, can be a perfect counterbalance to the earthiness of beets or the peppery kick of radishes.

Nutrition, however, is not just about vitamins and minerals; it's also about understanding the glycemic index of fruits, the fiber content in vegetables, and the overall impact of a juice concoction on one's body. A juice that spikes blood sugar might provide a burst of energy initially, but it can lead to a rapid drop in energy levels later on. Incorporating low-glycemic fruits and veggies, like berries or cucumbers, can help regulate this.

Additionally, the world of flavors is vast and diverse. There's no harm in experimenting with uncommon ingredients, like fennel or dandelion greens, both of which offer unique flavors and a plethora of health benefits. By broadening your ingredient spectrum, you not only enrich your taste experience but also diversify the nutrient profile of your juices.

In conclusion, balancing taste and nutrition is akin to composing a symphony. With every ingredient being a distinct note, it's up to the juicer—much like a maestro—to ensure that the final product is not only pleasing to the ears but also soul-stirring. Similarly, a well-balanced juice should not only tantalize the taste buds but also invigorate the body from within.

Color Theory in Juicing

In the art of juicing, understanding the color wheel is more than a visual delight—it's a guide to ensuring a diverse intake of nutrients.

The colors in fruits and vegetables are the result of specific phytonutrients, each with its own set of health benefits. Let's delve into the palette of nature and unravel the connection between the hues of our juices and their nutritional bounty.

Ruby Reds and Passionate Pinks: Ingredients like pomegranates, beets, and red grapes are rich in these shades. The red pigment often signals the presence of antioxidants like lycopene and anthocyanins. Lycopene, for instance, has been associated with heart health and a reduced risk of certain types of cancer.

Sunny Yellows and Oranges: These sunny shades, as seen in oranges, mangoes, and carrots, are often indicators of carotenoids like beta-carotene. Beta-carotene is a precursor to vitamin A, vital for vision, immune function, and skin health.

Deep Greens: Kale, spinach, and green apples lend a lush green shade to juices. Chlorophyll, the pigment responsible for this color, isn't the only star here. Green veggies are packed with an array of vitamins and minerals. They're especially rich in folate, iron, and calcium.

Mysterious Blues and Purples: Think blueberries, blackberries, and eggplants. These ingredients owe their deep colors to anthocyanins, powerful antioxidants that are known to support brain health and reduce inflammation.

Earthy Browns: Not the most visually appealing, perhaps, when compared to the vibrant colors, but ingredients like seeds, some nuts, and certain root vegetables can add a brownish tint. These are often rich in fiber, omega fatty acids, and various minerals.

When crafting juice recipes, considering color is like painting on a blank canvas. Combining a red strawberry with a blue blueberry not only results in a delightful purple hue but also merges the health benefits of both colors.
Moreover, a visually appealing juice can be more enticing, making the health journey a deliciously vibrant experience.

Maximizing Nutrient Absorption: Pairing Ingredients

In the realm of juicing, simply blending a variety of ingredients isn't the endgame. The ultimate goal is to ensure our bodies effectively absorb the plethora of nutrients from these ingredients. After all, the real magic happens when the vitamins, minerals, and antioxidants from our juice blend work synergistically within our bodies to promote optimal health.
Imagine you're hosting a dinner party. For the party to be a success, certain guests pair well together, creating memorable conversations and a lively ambiance. Similarly, certain ingredients in our juices amplify each other's nutritional benefits when paired correctly.

Iron and Vitamin C: One of the most classic and effective pairings is that of iron and vitamin C. While green leafy vegetables such as spinach and kale are excellent sources of non-heme iron, our body absorbs this type of iron better when it's paired with vitamin C. So, adding a splash of orange or a squeeze of lemon to a green juice can help unlock the maximum iron potential from those greens.

Turmeric and Black Pepper: Another intriguing pairing is that of turmeric and black pepper. Turmeric contains curcumin, a compound lauded for its anti-inflammatory properties. However, curcumin is not easily absorbed by our bodies. Enter black pepper. Piperine, a compound in black pepper, enhances the absorption of curcumin by a staggering 2000%. A pinch of ground black pepper in a carrot-turmeric juice can thus elevate its benefits.

Fats and Fat-Soluble Vitamins: Vitamins A, D, E, and K are fat-soluble, meaning they require fats to be absorbed efficiently. Incorporating avocados or a touch of cold-pressed flaxseed oil into juices that are rich in these vitamins can enhance their absorption. Think of a kale and spinach juice (rich in Vitamin K) with a hint of avocado. It's not just creamy; it's nutritionally optimized.

Avoiding Anti-nutrient Combinations: Just as some nutrients amplify each other, others can inhibit absorption. For example, the calcium in spinach can bind with the iron, reducing its absorption. While this doesn't negate the value of combining such ingredients occasionally, it's worth being aware of and planning around for maximum benefit.

Chapter 5: 30-Day Detailed Juicing Plan

Week 1Meal Plan

Day	Morning	Mid-Morning	Lunch	Mid-Afternoon	Evening
1	MORNING SUNRISE	GREEN DETOX DELIGHT	APPLE GINGER SPARK	DIGESTIVE DELIGHT	SWEET GREENS
2	TROPICAL LIFT	PINEAPPLE SUNRISE	SKIN RENEWAL	RADIANT ROSE REFRESH	PEARLICIOUS BOOST
3	ZESTY MINT RUSH	BERRY DETOX BLEND	LUCID LIME LIFT	LIVER LOVER	ELECTRIC ELDERBERRY ENERGIZER
4	BERRY BURST	ZEN ZUCCHINI ZEST	GUT RELIEF	HEARTY HEART	VIVID VEGGIE VIGOR
5	GREEN POWERHOUSE	PERSIMMON PEACH POTION	INVIGORATING IVORY INSIGHT	BONE BUILDER	SUBLIME STRAWBERRY SORBET
6	TANTALIZING TANGERINE TWIST	TOMATO TANGO	BRAIN BOOST	BOLD BLACKBERRY BLITZ	RUBY RED ROMANCE
7	CITRUS CLEANSE BOOST	DREAMY DRAGON DELIGHT	LUNG LIFTER	MANGO MERMAID MAGIC	VITAL VINEGAR VIBE

Daily Breakdown: Recipes, Goals, and Tips

Day 1 - Kickstarting Health:
- **Goals:** Initiate the detoxification process and invigorate your energy levels.
- **Tips:** MORNING SUNRISE has properties to give you an immediate energy boost. Drink plenty of water between juices.

Day 2 - Cellular Renewal:
- **Goals:** Focus on the rejuvenation of skin cells and improved digestion.
- **Tips:** PINEAPPLE SUNRISE is rich in bromelain, which aids in digestion.

Day 3 - Liver & Detox Focus:
- **Goals:** Support liver function and continue detox.
- **Tips:** Incorporate a light walk or yoga to complement the detox process.

Day 4 - Heart & Bone Health:
- **Goals:** Strengthen your cardiovascular system and enhance bone health.
- **Tips:** Include some light stretches to keep muscles flexible and joints healthy.

Day 5 - Digestion & Gut Health:
- **Goals:** Improve gut function and support overall digestion.
- **Tips:** Allow at least 30 minutes between each juice to let your digestive system process effectively.

Day 6 - Brain Boost & Immunity:
- **Goals:** Sharpen your cognitive abilities and reinforce the immune system.
- **Tips:** Engage in mental activities like puzzles or reading to stimulate the brain, and ensure you're getting adequate sleep to support immune function.

Day 7 - Balancing Act:
- **Goals:** Achieve a balanced state in both body and mind.
- **Tips:** MANGO MERMAID MAGIC contains a myriad of vitamins to balance your nutrient intake. Consider some meditation or deep breathing exercises to find mental balance.

Tracking Your Progress: Journal Prompts and Checklists
Journal Prompts:
- **Day 1:** How do you feel starting this journey? Any specific expectations?
- **Day 2:** Note any changes in your energy levels or digestion.
- **Day 3:** Are you experiencing any detox symptoms like headaches or fatigue?
- **Day 4:** How is your appetite between juices? Do you notice any changes in cravings?
- **Day 5:** Are you more in tune with your body's needs?
- **Day 6:** How is your mental clarity? Do you feel more focused?
- **Day 7:** Reflect on the past week. What were the highs and lows?

Checklists:
- Daily hydration (Aim for 8 glasses of water).
- Physical activity (At least 15 minutes daily).
- 5 minutes of deep breathing or meditation.
- Sleep tracking (Aim for 7-8 hours).

Adjusting the Plan for Personal Needs and Preferences
- **Taste Preferences:** If certain juices don't appeal to your taste buds, feel free to switch them with others from the list that align with your goals for the day.

- **Allergies or Sensitivities:** If you're allergic to any ingredients in a juice, substitute with a similar ingredient that doesn't cause reactions. For instance, if you're allergic to pineapples, you can opt for mango or papaya.
- **Intensity of the Plan:** If you feel too hungry, it's okay to add another juice or drink more of the same one, especially if it's a veggie-heavy blend.
- **Physical Activity:** If you're highly active or engaging in intense workouts, you might need more calories. Add a protein-rich nut milk or an avocado-based juice from the list.

Week 2 Meal Plan

Day	Morning	Mid-Morning	Lunch	Mid-Afternoon	Evening
8	MORNING SUNRISE	LUCID LIME LIFT	ELECTRIC ELDERBERRY ENERGIZER	ZEN ZUCCHINI ZEST	SUBLIME STRAWBERRY SORBET
9	TROPICAL LIFT	LUSCIOUS LYCHEE LUSH	GUT GLORY	RUBY RED ROMANCE	VIVID VEGGIE VIGOR
10	BERRY BURST	CRANBERRY BLISS	BRAIN BREEZE	ELECTRIC ESPRESSO ESCAPE	MIGRAINE MITIGATOR
11	APPLE GINGER SPARK	PEARLICIOUS BOOST	INFLAMMATION INSURGENT	SERENE SAGE SORBET	LIVER LOVER
12	ZESTY MINT RUSH	LAVENDER LEMONADE LIFT	VITAL VINEGAR VIBE	WHIMSICAL WATERMELON WHIRL	BONE BENEFACTOR
13	SUNNY SPIRIT STIMULATOR	GOLDEN GLOW	LUNG LIFTER	JAZZY JAVA JIVE	THYROID THRIVER
14	CUCUMBER REFRESH	RADIANT ROSE REFRESH	HEARTY HEART	FRESH FIG FANTASY	ADRENAL AID

Daily Breakdown: Recipes, Goals, and Tips

Day 8 - Morning Energy & Evening Calm:
- **Goals:** Boost energy to kick start the week and wind down in the evening for a restful sleep.

- **Tips:** Start your day with some light stretches and end with calming meditation.

Day 9 - Gut Health & Vibrancy:
- **Goals:** Foster a healthy digestive system and keep the body vibrant and energetic.
- **Tips:** Consider practicing yoga poses that aid digestion and keep yourself hydrated.

Day 10 - Brain Clarity & Relief:
- **Goals:** Maintain focus and relieve any headaches or migraines.
- **Tips:** Take short breaks every hour to rest your eyes and mind if you're working on a screen.

Day 11 - Inflammation Control & Liver Health:
- **Goals:** Reduce inflammation and support liver function.
- **Tips:** Avoid processed foods and alcohol to give your liver a break.

Day 12 - Nutrient Balance & Bone Health:
- **Goals:** Ensure a balanced intake of essential nutrients and support bone health.
- **Tips:** Enjoy some sun for a dose of vitamin D, which is beneficial for bones.

Day 13 - Respiratory Support & Thyroid Health:
- **Goals:** Aid the respiratory system and ensure thyroid functionality.
- **Tips:** Try deep breathing exercises or even a short walk in a park.

Day 14 - Cardio Health & Adrenal Support:
- **Goals:** Foster a strong cardiovascular system and assist adrenal health for stress management.
- **Tips:** Engage in a moderate aerobic activity like brisk walking or cycling. Practice stress-relieving techniques such as mindfulness or deep breathing.

Tracking Your Progress: Journal Prompts and Checklists
Journal Prompts:
- How did the flavors of this week's juices impact your mood and energy levels?
- Were there any days you felt particularly energetic or sluggish?
- Did you notice any physical changes or improvements in any specific health areas, like digestion or skin health?
- How are you feeling mentally, especially in terms of clarity and focus?
- Were there any particular ingredients or recipes you really enjoyed or disliked?

Checklists:
- Rate each day's energy level from 1-10.
- Note any new or unusual physical sensations or changes.
- Track hours of sleep each night.

- Document daily water intake.
- List any additional foods or snacks consumed.

Adjusting the Plan for Personal Needs and Preferences

While the plan provides a comprehensive approach to a balanced and healthy juice intake, it's essential to listen to your body and adjust accordingly. Here are some suggestions:

1. **Variety:** If you find a particular juice flavor or ingredient not to your taste, feel free to swap it with another from the list. Ensure you're getting a mix of nutrients.
2. **Intensity:** If you find a juice too strong or intense, consider diluting it with some water or adding a milder ingredient, such as cucumber or celery.
3. **Health Needs:** For specific health concerns, focus on juices that target that area. For example, if you have digestive issues, prioritize juices like GUT GLORY and DIGESTIVE DYNAMO.
4. **Additional Nutrition:** If you're feeling particularly hungry or lacking in energy, consider adding a protein-rich smoothie or a small, healthy snack to your day.
5. **Feedback:** Keeping a journal, as mentioned, can provide insights into how certain juices affect you. This feedback can guide adjustments to the plan based on your unique reactions and preferences.

Week 3 Meal Plan

Day	Morning	Mid-Morning	Lunch	Mid-Afternoon	Evening
Day 15	ZEN ZUCCHINI ZEST	ELECTRIC ELDERBERRY ENERGIZER	GOLDEN GLOW GOURMET	JUBILANT JICAMA JOLT	JOINT JUBILEE
Day 16	DREAMY DRAGON DELIGHT	BOLD BLACKBERRY BLITZ	RUBY RED ROMANCE	VIVID VEGGIE VIGOR	LIVER LUMINARY
Day 17	WHIMSICAL WATERMELON WHIRL	BLOSSOMING BLUEBERRY BLAST	SPICY KICKSTART	PINEAPPLE SUNRISE	BONE BENEFACTOR
Day 18	PEARLICIOUS BOOST	FIERY FIG FERVOR	MORNING SUNRISE	RADIANT ROSE REFRESH	BRAIN BREEZE
Day 19	MANGO MERMAID MAGIC	ELECTRIC ESPRESSO ESCAPE	GREEN POWERHOUSE	SWEET GREENS	LUNG LEVITATOR
Day 20	LUSCIOUS LYCHEE LUSH	NECTAROUS NUTMEG NUDGE	TROPICAL LIFT	APPLE GINGER SPARK	INFLAMMATION INSURGENT
Day 21	SUBLIME STRAWBERRY SORBET	VIVACIOUS VANILLA VITALIZER	ZESTY MINT RUSH	CRANBERRY BLISS	KIDNEY CLEANSER

Daily Breakdown: Recipes, Goals, and Tips

Day 15 - Zesty Detox & Evening Soothing:
- **Goals**: Start your day with a detoxifying boost and soothe your body in the evening, preparing it for quality sleep.
- **Tips**: Consider a morning jog to enhance the detox process and finish your day with a warm, relaxing bath.

Day 16 - Fruity Mornings & Liver Love:
- **Goals**: Energize your morning with fruity flavors and focus on liver health in the evening.
- **Tips**: Pair your morning juice with a sunrise walk. For the evening, practice deep breathing exercises to enhance liver detoxification.

Day 17 - Hydration & Bone Strengthening:

- **Goals**: Prioritize hydration early in the day and strengthen the bones as you wrap it up.
- **Tips**: Drink a glass of water before your morning juice. In the evening, indulge in gentle stretches to complement the bone-strengthening benefits of your juice.

Day 18 - Creamy Start & Brainy Endings:

- **Goals**: Enjoy a creamy, comforting start and focus on cognitive health in the evening.
- **Tips**: Start your day with a gratitude journaling session and end it with puzzles or brain games to maximize the cognitive benefits of your juices.

Day 19 - Tropical Day & Respiratory Relief:

- **Goals**: Bask in tropical vibes throughout the day and focus on lung health in the evening.
- **Tips**: Enjoy your morning juice outdoors, preferably in nature. In the evening, practice deep breathing exercises to optimize respiratory health.

Day 20 - Vitamin C Boost & Kidney Care:

- **Goals**: Amplify your Vitamin C intake during the day and cater to kidney health in the evening.
- **Tips**: Pair your morning juice with a sunbathing session for natural Vitamin D. For the evening, practice foot massages, as feet have pressure points linked to kidney health.

Day 21 - Berry Bliss & Kidney Maintenance:

- **Goals**: Revel in the antioxidant-rich benefits of berries during the day and continue with kidney care in the evening.
- **Tips**: Complement your morning juice with berry-infused water throughout the day. For the evening, ensure you're maintaining a balance in fluid intake to aid the kidney cleanse.

Tracking Your Progress: Journal Prompts and Checklists
Journal Prompts:
- How did the flavors of this week's juices impact your mood and energy levels?
- Were there any days you felt particularly energetic or sluggish?
- Did you notice any physical changes or improvements in any specific health areas, like digestion or skin health?
- How are you feeling mentally, especially in terms of clarity and focus?
- Were there any particular ingredients or recipes you really enjoyed or disliked?

Checklists:
- Rate each day's energy level from 1-10.
- Note any new or unusual physical sensations or changes.

- Track hours of sleep each night.
- Document daily water intake.
- List any additional foods or snacks consumed.

Week 4 Meal Plan

Day	Morning	Mid-Morning	Lunch	Mid-Afternoon	Evening
22	GREEN DETOX DELIGHT	CITRUS CLEANSE BOOST	BERRY DETOX BLEND	MINTY MELON FLUSH	HERBAL REFRESH CLEANSE
23	TROPICAL CLEANSE WAVE	BERRY DETOX BLEND	SPICY GREEN DETOX	CARROT KICK-START	ZESTY BEETROOT BOOST
24	PINEAPPLE SUNRISE	CRANBERRY BLISS	LUSCIOUS LYCHEE LUSH	VELVET VIBRANCE	MANGO MERMAID MAGIC
25	RUBY RED ROMANCE	LAVENDER LEMONADE LIFT	CITRUS SEA BREEZE	PEARL OF THE ORIENT	TANTALIZING TANGERINE TWIST
26	GOLDEN GLOW GOURMET	BLOSSOMING BLUEBERRY BLAST	FRESH FIG FANTASY	DREAMY DRAGON DELIGHT	WHIMSICAL WATERMELON WHIRL
27	ZEN ZUCCHINI ZEST	GREEN POWERHOUSE	TROPICAL LIFT	BERRY BURST	APPLE GINGER SPARK
28	SPICY KICKSTART	PEARLICIOUS BOOST	LUCID LIME LIFT	RADIANT RASPBERRY RALLY	VIVACIOUS VANILLA VITALIZER

Daily Breakdown: Recipes, Goals, and Tips

Day 22 - Herbal Detox & Evening Glow:
- **Goals:** Commence the week with a herby detox and let your skin glow by the evening.
- **Tips:** Engage in a morning yoga session to aid detoxification. For the evening, consider a face mask to enhance the glowing effect.

Day 23 - Citrus Radiance & Tomato Tranquility:
- **Goals:** Amplify your Vitamin C levels with citrus in the morning and soothe your senses with the calming effects of tomatoes in the evening.

- **Tips:** Boost your morning routine with a brisk walk. In the evening, indulge in a tomato-based meal or salad to complement the juice.

Day 24 - Beetroot Boost & Tropical Tunes:
- **Goals:** Rejuvenate with the earthiness of beets during the day and sail into a tropical mood as the evening unfolds.
- **Tips:** For the morning, consider a countryside walk. By evening, let the tropical vibes guide you into a light dance session.

Day 25 - Refreshing Mornings & Euphoric Evenings:
- **Goals:** Begin your day with a refreshed spirit and let euphoria take over by evening.
- **Tips:** Pair your morning juice with some mindfulness meditation. As night falls, let loose and embrace the euphoric vibes with your favorite calming music.

Day 26 - Berry Beginnings & Sunset Soothers:
- **Goals:** Dive into a berry-filled day and smoothly transition into soothing sunset flavors.
- **Tips:** Enjoy a morning filled with nature – perhaps a hike. As the day wraps up, relax on your balcony or garden, enjoying the sunset.

Day 27 - Dreamy Flavors & Zen Moments:
- **Goals:** Float through your day with dreamy juice flavors and end with a serene zen state.
- **Tips:** Your morning juice pairs well with a relaxing bath. For the evening, embrace Zen practices like deep meditation or calming tea rituals.

Day 28 - Energy Amplifiers & Digestive Delights:
- **Goals:** Charge your body's energy reserves throughout the day and ensure a digestive delight by evening.
- **Tips:** Along with your morning juice, engage in high-energy activities like aerobics. By evening, wind down with gentle belly massages.

Chapter 6: Specialized Juicing Regimens

Detox and Cleanse Juices

GREEN DETOX DELIGHT

P.T.: 10 minutes
SERVES: 1
INGR.:
- 1 large cucumber
- 2 kale leaves
- 1 lemon, peeled
- 1 inch ginger root
- 1 green apple

PROCEDURE:
1. Wash all the ingredients thoroughly.
2. Peel the lemon and remove seeds from the apple.
3. Chop the ingredients into juicer-friendly pieces.
4. Feed the ingredients through the juicer one at a time.
5. Serve immediately over ice, if desired.

NUTRITIONAL VALUES: 80 calories, 0.5g fat, 20g carbs, 2g protein, 3g fiber, 10g sugar.

CITRUS CLEANSE BOOST

P.T.: 7 minutes
SERVES: 1
INGR.:
- 2 oranges, peeled
- 1 grapefruit, peeled
- 1/2 lemon, peeled
- 1 carrot
- 1 inch turmeric root

PROCEDURE:
1. Thoroughly wash the carrot and turmeric root.
2. Peel all citrus fruits.
3. Cut fruits into manageable sizes for juicing.
4. Juice all ingredients together.
5. Serve immediately, stirring well before drinking.

NUTRITIONAL VALUES: 90 calories, 0.3g fat, 22g carbs, 2g protein, 4g fiber, 12g sugar.

BERRY DETOX BLEND

P.T.: 10 minutes
SERVES: 1
INGR.:
- 1 cup blueberries
- 1 cup raspberries
- 1/2 beetroot

- 1/2 lemon, peeled
- 1 inch ginger root

PROCEDURE:
1. Wash all ingredients.
2. Chop beetroot and ginger into small pieces.
3. Add all ingredients to the juicer.
4. Process until smooth and thoroughly combined.
5. Pour into a glass and enjoy immediately.

NUTRITIONAL VALUES: 95 calories, 0.7g fat, 23g carbs, 2.5g protein, 5g fiber, 13g sugar.

TROPICAL CLEANSE WAVE

P.T.: 8 minutes
SERVES: 1
INGR.:
- 1/2 pineapple, peeled and cored
- 1 kiwi
- 1/2 lime, peeled
- 1 small cucumber
- 1 inch aloe vera leaf

PROCEDURE:
1. Wash and prepare all fruits.
2. Slice the aloe vera leaf and extract the gel inside.
3. Place all ingredients into the juicer.
4. Process until all ingredients are juiced and mixed well.
5. Pour and relish the tropical flavors.

NUTRITIONAL VALUES: 100 calories, 0.5g fat, 24g carbs, 2g protein, 3g fiber, 15g sugar.

MINTY MELON FLUSH

P.T.: 6 minutes
SERVES: 1
INGR.:
- 1 cup watermelon chunks
- 1/2 cup honeydew melon chunks
- 1/2 cup cantaloupe chunks
- 1/2 lime, peeled
- 8 fresh mint leaves

PROCEDURE:
1. Prepare all the melons by removing seeds and cutting into chunks.
2. Add melon pieces, lime, and mint leaves into the juicer.
3. Juice until all ingredients are combined smoothly.
4. Serve chilled and enjoy the refreshing taste.

NUTRITIONAL VALUES: 85 calories, 0.2g fat, 21g carbs, 1g protein, 1g fiber, 18g sugar.

SPICY GREEN DETOX

P.T.: 7 minutes
SERVES: 1
INGR.:

- 2 celery stalks
- 1 green apple
- 1/2 lemon, peeled
- 1 cup spinach
- 1/4 jalapeño (deseeded)

PROCEDURE:

1. Wash and prepare all ingredients.
2. Begin juicing with celery followed by the other ingredients.
3. Process until the juice is smooth and combined.
4. Pour into a glass and savor the spicy kick.

NUTRITIONAL VALUES: 70 calories, 0.4g fat, 17g carbs, 2g protein, 3g fiber, 11g sugar.

HERBAL REFRESH CLEANSE

P.T.: 9 minutes
SERVES: 1
INGR.:

- 1 pear
- 1 inch ginger root
- 1/2 cucumber
- 1/2 lemon, peeled
- A handful of fresh basil leaves

PROCEDURE:

1. Wash all ingredients thoroughly.
2. Slice pear and cucumber into manageable pieces.
3. Place all ingredients into the juicer.
4. Juice until well combined.
5. Sip and enjoy the harmonious blend of flavors.

NUTRITIONAL VALUES: 80 calories, 0.3g fat, 20g carbs, 1g protein, 4g fiber, 12g sugar.

CARROT KICK-START

P.T.: 7 minutes
SERVES: 1
INGR.:

- 4 carrots
- 1/2 apple
- 1 inch ginger root
- 1/2 lemon, peeled
- A pinch of cayenne pepper

PROCEDURE:

1. Wash and chop the carrots and apple.
2. Begin juicing with carrots, then add the apple, ginger, and lemon.
3. Once juiced, stir in a pinch of cayenne pepper for a slight kick.
4. Serve immediately and relish the spicy-sweet flavors.

NUTRITIONAL VALUES: 85 calories, 0.5g fat, 20g carbs, 1.5g protein, 4g fiber, 10g sugar.

TOMATO TANGO

P.T.: 8 minutes
SERVES: 1
INGR.:

- 3 ripe tomatoes
- 1/4 red bell pepper
- 1/2 lemon, peeled
- A pinch of Himalayan pink salt
- 1 celery stalk

PROCEDURE:

1. Prepare tomatoes by washing and removing the stems.
2. Juice tomatoes, red bell pepper, and celery.
3. Squeeze in the lemon and add a pinch of salt.
4. Mix well and serve for a savory cleanse.

NUTRITIONAL VALUES: 70 calories, 0.7g fat, 15g carbs, 2g protein, 3g fiber, 9g sugar.

ZESTY BEETROOT BOOST

P.T.: 10 minutes
SERVES: 1
INGR.:

- 1 medium beetroot
- 1 carrot
- 1/2 orange, peeled
- 1 inch ginger root
- 1/2 lemon, peeled

PROCEDURE:

1. Wash and prepare beetroot, carrot, and ginger.
2. Start the juicing process with beetroot, followed by carrot and ginger.
3. Add orange and lemon last.
4. Process until smooth and serve immediately for a zesty detoxifying experience.

NUTRITIONAL VALUES: 95 calories, 0.4g fat, 22g carbs, 2.5g protein, 5g fiber, 14g sugar.

CITRUS SEA BREEZE

P.T.: 7 minutes
SERVES: 1
INGR.:

- 1 grapefruit, peeled
- 1/2 lemon, peeled
- 1/2 lime, peeled
- 1 orange, peeled
- A pinch of sea salt

PROCEDURE:

1. Start the juicing process with grapefruit.
2. Continue with lemon, lime, and finish with the orange.
3. Once fully juiced, stir in a pinch of sea salt.
4. Serve immediately, preferably chilled, for a refreshing detox experience.

NUTRITIONAL VALUES: 90 calories, 0.3g fat, 22g carbs, 1.7g protein, 3g fiber, 18g sugar.

PINEAPPLE SUNRISE

P.T.: 10 minutes
SERVES: 2
INGR:

- 1 pineapple, peeled and sliced
- 2 kiwis
- A thumb-sized piece of ginger
- 1 lime, peeled
- A pinch of turmeric powder

PROCEDURE:

1. Begin by washing and preparing all ingredients.
2. Feed the pineapple, kiwi, ginger, and lime through the juicer.
3. Stir in a pinch of turmeric powder.
4. Serve immediately.
5. Can be refrigerated for up to 24 hours.

NUTRITIONAL VALUES: Rich in vitamin C, bromelain, and antioxidants.

CRANBERRY BLISS

P.T.: 10 minutes
SERVES: 2
INGR:

- 2 cups fresh cranberries
- 2 apples
- 1 orange, peeled
- 1 pear
- 1-inch piece of ginger

PROCEDURE:

1. Wash and prepare the ingredients.
2. Juice cranberries, apples, orange, pear, and ginger.
3. Stir thoroughly and serve immediately.
4. For best results, drink on an empty stomach.
5. If too tart, consider diluting with water or adding a natural sweetener.

NUTRITIONAL VALUES: High in vitamin C, dietary fiber, and anti-inflammatory properties.

LUSCIOUS LYCHEE LUSH

P.T.: 8 minutes
SERVES: 2
INGR:

- 2 cups lychees, peeled and deseeded
- 1 cucumber
- 1 lemon, peeled
- 5 fresh mint leaves
- A pinch of Himalayan pink salt

PROCEDURE:

1. Wash and prepare the ingredients.
2. Process lychees, cucumber, lemon, and mint leaves through the juicer.
3. Stir in a pinch of Himalayan pink salt.
4. Pour into glasses and serve chilled.
5. Garnish with a mint sprig if desired.

NUTRITIONAL VALUES: Rich in vitamin C, B-complex vitamins, and anti-inflammatory properties.

PEARL OF THE ORIENT

P.T.: 10 minutes
SERVES: 2
INGR:

- 3 pears
- 2 stalks of celery
- 1 cucumber
- 1 lemon, peeled
- A sprinkle of chia seeds

PROCEDURE:

1. Thoroughly wash and prepare the ingredients.
2. Juice pears, celery, cucumber, and lemon.
3. Pour into glasses.
4. Sprinkle with chia seeds.
5. Stir and serve immediately.

NUTRITIONAL VALUES: High in dietary fiber, vitamin K, and hydration properties.

VELVET VIBRANCE

P.T.: 10 minutes
SERVES: 2
INGR:

- 2 beetroots
- 1 apple
- 2 carrots
- 1-inch piece of ginger
- A dash of cayenne pepper

PROCEDURE:

1. Prepare and wash all ingredients.
2. Juice beetroots, apple, carrots, and ginger.
3. Pour into glasses.
4. Add a dash of cayenne pepper for a spicy kick.
5. Stir well and serve immediately.

NUTRITIONAL VALUES: Rich in antioxidants, beta-carotene, and detoxifying properties.

MANGO MERMAID MAGIC

P.T.: 10 minutes
SERVES: 2
INGR:

- 2 ripe mangoes, peeled and pitted
- 1 orange, peeled
- 1/2 a small papaya
- 5 fresh basil leaves
- A splash of coconut water

PROCEDURE:

1. Prepare all the ingredients.
2. Juice mangoes, orange, and papaya.
3. Pour the juice into a blender, add basil leaves and blend until smooth.
4. Add a splash of coconut water for added hydration.
5. Serve chilled with a basil garnish.

NUTRITIONAL VALUES: High in vitamins A, C, and digestive enzymes.

RUBY RED ROMANCE

P.T.: 10 minutes
SERVES: 2
INGR:

- 2 grapefruits, peeled
- 1 cup strawberries
- 1/2 a lime, peeled
- 1 small beetroot
- A pinch of pink Himalayan salt

PROCEDURE:

1. Wash and prepare all the ingredients.
2. Juice grapefruits, strawberries, lime, and beetroot.
3. Pour into glasses.
4. Add a pinch of pink Himalayan salt for a unique flavor twist.
5. Stir well and serve immediately.

NUTRITIONAL VALUES: Rich in vitamin C, antioxidants, and immune-boosting properties.

LAVENDER LEMONADE LIFT

P.T.: 12 minutes
SERVES: 2
INGR:

- 3 lemons, peeled
- 2 cups of water
- 2 tbsp honey or agave nectar
- 1 drop of edible lavender essential oil (optional)
- Ice cubes

PROCEDURE:

1. Juice the lemons.
2. Mix the lemon juice with water, sweetener of choice, and a drop of lavender oil in a pitcher.
3. Pour into glasses filled with ice cubes.
4. Stir gently and enjoy the refreshing taste.
5. Garnish with a slice of lemon or a sprig of fresh lavender.

NUTRITIONAL VALUES: Rich in vitamin C, hydration, and calming properties from the lavender.

RADIANT ROSE REFRESH

P.T.: 10 minutes
SERVES: 2
INGR:

- 1 apple
- 1 pear
- 1 cup of fresh rose petals (ensure they're edible/organic)
- 1/2 a lemon, peeled
- A drop of rosewater (optional)

PROCEDURE:

1. Wash and prepare the ingredients.
2. Juice apple, pear, rose petals, and lemon.
3. Pour into glasses.
4. Add a drop of rosewater for enhanced aroma.
5. Stir and enjoy immediately.

NUTRITIONAL VALUES: High in dietary fiber, vitamin C, and skin-enhancing properties.

TANTALIZING TANGERINE TWIST

P.T.: 8 minutes
SERVES: 2
INGR:

- 4 tangerines, peeled
- 1 grapefruit, peeled
- A small piece of turmeric root
- 1/2 a lime, peeled
- A dash of black pepper

PROCEDURE:

1. Prepare and wash all ingredients.
2. Juice tangerines, grapefruit, turmeric, and lime.
3. Pour the juice into glasses.
4. Add a dash of black pepper to activate the turmeric's beneficial properties.
5. Stir well and serve immediately.

NUTRITIONAL VALUES: Rich in vitamin C, anti-inflammatory properties, and antioxidants.

SERENE SAGE SORBET

P.T.: 12 minutes
SERVES: 2
INGR:

- 2 green apples
- 1 cucumber
- 1/2 a lemon, peeled
- 5 fresh sage leaves
- A splash of sparkling water

PROCEDURE:

1. Wash and prepare the ingredients.
2. Juice the apples, cucumber, lemon, and sage leaves.
3. Pour into glasses.
4. Top with a splash of sparkling water for a fizzy feel.
5. Garnish with a slice of lemon or a sprig of sage.

NUTRITIONAL VALUES: High in dietary fiber, vitamin C, and relaxation properties from the sage.

EXOTIC ELDERBERRY EUPHORIA

P.T.: 10 minutes
SERVES: 2
INGR:

- 1 cup elderberries
- 2 plums
- 1/2 a lemon, peeled
- 1-inch piece of ginger
- A sprinkle of flaxseeds

PROCEDURE:

1. Thoroughly wash and prepare the ingredients.
2. Juice elderberries, plums, lemon, and ginger.
3. Pour into glasses.
4. Sprinkle with flaxseeds for added texture and nutritional boost.
5. Stir and enjoy immediately.

NUTRITIONAL VALUES: Rich in antioxidants, vitamin C, and omega-3 fatty acids.

GOLDEN GLOW GOURMET

P.T.: 8 minutes
SERVES: 2
INGR:

- 2 oranges, peeled
- 1 carrot
- A thumb-sized piece of turmeric
- 1/2 a lemon, peeled
- A sprinkle of black sesame seeds

PROCEDURE:

1. Wash and prepare the ingredients.
2. Juice the oranges, carrot, turmeric, and lemon.
3. Pour the juice into glasses.

4. Sprinkle with black sesame seeds for a unique look and added health benefits.
5. Serve immediately.

NUTRITIONAL VALUES: High in vitamin C, beta-carotene, and anti-inflammatory properties.

BLOSSOMING BLUEBERRY BLAST

P.T.: 10 minutes
SERVES: 2
INGR:
- 1 cup blueberries
- 1 apple
- 2 kiwis
- 1/2 a lime, peeled
- A pinch of Himalayan pink salt

PROCEDURE:
1. Prepare and wash all ingredients.
2. Juice the blueberries, apple, kiwis, and lime.
3. Pour into glasses.
4. Add a pinch of Himalayan pink salt for a flavor boost.
5. Stir and enjoy.

NUTRITIONAL VALUES: Rich in antioxidants, vitamin C, and minerals.

FRESH FIG FANTASY

P.T.: 10 minutes
SERVES: 2
INGR:
- 4 fresh figs
- 2 pears
- 1/2 a lime, peeled
- A thumb-sized piece of ginger
- A splash of coconut water

PROCEDURE:
1. Wash and prepare the ingredients.
2. Juice the figs, pears, lime, and ginger.
3. Pour the juice into glasses.
4. Add a splash of coconut water for added hydration.
5. Stir and serve immediately.

NUTRITIONAL VALUES: High in dietary fiber, vitamins, and hydration properties.

PERSIMMON PEACH POTION

P.T.: 10 minutes
SERVES: 2
INGR:
- 2 ripe persimmons
- 1 peach
- 1 orange, peeled
- 1-inch piece of ginger
- A sprinkle of chia seeds

PROCEDURE:
1. Prepare and wash all ingredients.
2. Juice persimmons, peach, orange, and ginger.
3. Pour into glasses.
4. Sprinkle with chia seeds for a nutrient boost.
5. Stir and enjoy immediately.

NUTRITIONAL VALUES: Rich in vitamin A, C, dietary fiber, and omega-3 fatty acids.

VELVET VIOLET VITALITY

P.T.: 10 minutes
SERVES: 2
INGR:

- 1 cup of blackberries
- 1 apple
- 2 stalks of celery
- 1/2 a lemon, peeled
- A splash of almond milk

PROCEDURE:

1. Wash and prepare the ingredients.
2. Juice blackberries, apple, celery, and lemon.
3. Pour the juice into glasses.
4. Add a splash of almond milk for a creamy touch.
5. Stir and serve immediately.

NUTRITIONAL VALUES: High in vitamin C, fiber, and calcium.

SUBLIME STRAWBERRY SORBET

P.T.: 8 minutes
SERVES: 2
INGR:

- 2 cups strawberries
- 1 kiwi
- 1/2 a lemon, peeled
- A thumb-sized piece of ginger
- A pinch of sea salt

PROCEDURE:

1. Prepare and wash all ingredients.
2. Juice strawberries, kiwi, lemon, and ginger.
3. Pour into glasses.
4. Add a pinch of sea salt to enhance flavors.
5. Stir well and serve immediately.

NUTRITIONAL VALUES: Rich in vitamin C, dietary fiber, and anti-inflammatory properties.

DREAMY DRAGON DELIGHT

P.T.: 10 minutes
SERVES: 2
INGR:

- 1 dragon fruit, peeled
- 1 apple
- 1 orange, peeled
- A thumb-sized piece of ginger
- A sprinkle of pumpkin seeds

PROCEDURE:

1. Wash and prepare the ingredients.
2. Juice dragon fruit, apple, orange, and ginger.
3. Pour the juice into glasses.
4. Sprinkle with pumpkin seeds for a crunch.
5. Enjoy immediately.

NUTRITIONAL VALUES: High in vitamin C, fiber, and magnesium.

WHIMSICAL WATERMELON WHIRL

P.T.: 10 minutes
SERVES: 2
INGR:

- 1/2 a small watermelon, peeled and deseeded
- 1/2 a lime, peeled
- A thumb-sized piece of ginger
- 5 fresh basil leaves
- A splash of sparkling water

PROCEDURE:

1. Prepare and wash all ingredients.
2. Juice watermelon, lime, ginger, and basil leaves.
3. Pour into glasses.
4. Top with a splash of sparkling water for a refreshing fizz.
5. Garnish with a basil sprig and enjoy.

NUTRITIONAL VALUES: Rich in hydration properties, vitamins, and anti-inflammatory benefits.

ZEN ZUCCHINI ZEST

P.T.: 8 minutes
SERVES: 2
INGR:

- 2 zucchinis
- 1 green apple
- 1/2 a lemon, peeled
- 1-inch piece of ginger
- A pinch of black pepper

PROCEDURE:

1. Wash and prepare the ingredients.
2. Juice zucchinis, apple, lemon, and ginger.
3. Pour the juice into glasses.
4. Add a pinch of black pepper for a flavor kick.
5. Stir and serve immediately.

NUTRITIONAL VALUES: High in dietary fiber, vitamin C, and anti-inflammatory properties.

Energy-Boosting Formulas

MORNING SUNRISE

P.T.: 6 minutes
SERVES: 1
INGR.:

- 1 carrot, peeled
- 1 apple, cored
- 1-inch piece of ginger
- 1 beet, peeled
- 2 celery stalks

PROCEDURE:

1. Begin juicing with the carrot and apple.
2. Add in the ginger, beet, and finish with celery.
3. Mix the juice well to combine the flavors.
4. Serve immediately and enjoy the invigorating taste.

NUTRITIONAL VALUES: 105 calories, 0.5g fat, 26g carbs, 2.5g protein, 5g fiber, 17g sugar.

GREEN POWERHOUSE

P.T.: 6 minutes
SERVES: 1
INGR.:

- 2 kale leaves
- 1 cucumber
- 1 green apple, cored
- 1/2 lemon, peeled
- A pinch of cayenne pepper

PROCEDURE:

1. Start with juicing kale and cucumber.
2. Follow with the green apple and lemon.
3. Stir in the cayenne pepper for an extra kick.
4. Serve immediately for a burst of energy.

NUTRITIONAL VALUES: 85 calories, 0.7g fat, 21g carbs, 2.9g protein, 4g fiber, 14g sugar.

TROPICAL LIFT

P.T.: 5 minutes

SERVES: 1

INGR.:

- 1/2 pineapple, peeled and cored
- 1 mango, peeled
- 1 passion fruit
- 1 kiwi, peeled
- 1-inch piece of turmeric

PROCEDURE:

1. Juice the pineapple and mango.
2. Add in the passion fruit, kiwi, and turmeric.
3. Blend well to combine the tropical flavors.
4. Serve immediately for a refreshing energy boost.

NUTRITIONAL VALUES: 110 calories, 0.8g fat, 27g carbs, 2.3g protein, 4g fiber, 20g sugar.

ZESTY MINT RUSH

P.T.: 5 minutes

SERVES: 1

INGR.:

- 2 oranges, peeled
- 1 handful of fresh mint leaves
- 1/2 lemon, peeled
- 1-inch piece of ginger
- 1 carrot, peeled

PROCEDURE:

1. Start with juicing the oranges and mint.
2. Add in the lemon, ginger, and carrot.
3. Mix well for a combined zest.
4. Serve immediately to awaken your senses.

NUTRITIONAL VALUES: 90 calories, 0.4g fat, 23g carbs, 1.8g protein, 4g fiber, 16g sugar.

BERRY BURST

P.T.: 5 minutes

SERVES: 1

INGR.:

- 1 handful of blueberries
- 1 handful of raspberries
- 1 handful of strawberries
- 1 apple, cored
- 1/2 lemon, peeled

PROCEDURE:

1. Begin by juicing all the berries.
2. Add in the apple and lemon.
3. Mix thoroughly to bring out the berry flavors.
4. Serve immediately for a quick energy surge.

NUTRITIONAL VALUES: 95 calories, 0.5g fat, 24g carbs, 1.5g protein, 4.5g fiber, 17g sugar.

APPLE GINGER SPARK

P.T.: 5 minutes
SERVES: 1
INGR.:

- 2 apples, cored
- 1-inch piece of ginger
- 1 pear, cored
- 1/2 lemon, peeled
- 1 carrot, peeled

PROCEDURE:

1. Begin with the apples and ginger.
2. Add in the pear, lemon, and carrot.
3. Blend to combine the ingredients well.
4. Serve immediately, preferably chilled.

NUTRITIONAL VALUES: 100 calories, 0.6g fat, 25g carbs, 1.6g protein, 5g fiber, 18g sugar.

SPICY KICKSTART

P.T.: 5 minutes
SERVES: 1
INGR.:

- 1 tomato
- 1/2 red bell pepper
- 1/2 jalapeño (deseeded if you prefer less heat)
- 1 celery stalk
- 1/2 lemon, peeled

PROCEDURE:

1. Start by juicing the tomato and red bell pepper.
2. Add in the jalapeño, celery, and lemon.
3. Stir well to incorporate all flavors.
4. Serve immediately for a spicy energy jolt.

NUTRITIONAL VALUES: 65 calories, 0.3g fat, 16g carbs, 2g protein, 4g fiber, 11g sugar.

CUCUMBER REFRESH

P.T.: 5 minutes
SERVES: 1
INGR.:

- 2 cucumbers
- 1/2 lime, peeled
- 1-inch piece of ginger
- 1 celery stalk
- 1 handful of fresh parsley

PROCEDURE:

1. Begin with juicing the cucumbers and lime.
2. Add in the ginger, celery, and parsley.
3. Stir to blend the ingredients properly.
4. Serve immediately for a revitalizing lift.

NUTRITIONAL VALUES: 70 calories, 0.4g fat, 17g carbs, 2.4g protein, 3g fiber, 10g sugar.

SWEET GREENS

P.T.: 6 minutes
SERVES: 1
INGR.:

- 1 handful of spinach
- 2 kiwis, peeled
- 1 green apple, cored
- 1 celery stalk
- 1-inch piece of ginger

PROCEDURE:

1. Start with the spinach and kiwis.
2. Continue with the green apple, celery, and ginger.
3. Mix thoroughly to blend the flavors.
4. Serve immediately for a pleasant energy boost.

NUTRITIONAL VALUES: 85 calories, 0.6g fat, 21g carbs, 2.5g protein, 4g fiber, 14g sugar.

PEARLICIOUS BOOST

P.T.: 6 minutes
SERVES: 1
INGR.:

- 2 pears, cored
- 1-inch piece of ginger
- 1 celery stalk
- 1/2 lemon, peeled
- A pinch of cinnamon

PROCEDURE:

1. Begin by juicing the pears and ginger.
2. Add in the celery and lemon.
3. Stir in the cinnamon for a touch of spice.
4. Serve immediately to kickstart your day.

NUTRITIONAL VALUES: 95 calories, 0.5g fat, 25g carbs, 1.2g protein, 6g fiber, 18g sugar.

GOLDEN GLOW

P.T.: 6 minutes
SERVES: 1
INGR.:

- 1 carrot, peeled
- 1 apple, cored
- 1-inch piece of turmeric
- 1/2 lemon, peeled
- 1-inch piece of ginger

PROCEDURE:

1. Start by juicing the carrot and apple.
2. Incorporate the turmeric and ginger next.
3. Finish with the lemon, ensuring the zesty flavor shines through.
4. Stir everything for a homogeneous mix.
5. Serve immediately to imbibe its golden energy.

NUTRITIONAL VALUES: 95 calories, 0.4g fat, 23g carbs, 1.3g protein, 5g fiber, 16g sugar.

LUCID LIME LIFT

P.T.: 10 minutes
SERVES: 2
INGR:

- 2 limes, peeled
- 1 green apple
- A handful of spinach
- 1-inch piece of ginger
- A pinch of cayenne pepper

PROCEDURE:

1. Prepare and wash all ingredients.
2. Juice limes, apple, spinach, and ginger.
3. Pour into glasses.
4. Add a pinch of cayenne for a kick.
5. Stir and serve immediately.

NUTRITIONAL VALUES: Rich in vitamin C, iron, and metabolism-boosting properties.

SUNNY SPIRIT STIMULATOR

P.T.: 9 minutes
SERVES: 2
INGR:

- 2 oranges, peeled
- 1 carrot
- 1/2 a grapefruit, peeled
- A thumb-sized piece of turmeric
- 1 teaspoon of honey

PROCEDURE:

1. Wash and prepare the ingredients.
2. Juice oranges, carrot, grapefruit, and turmeric together.
3. Stir in honey until dissolved.
4. Pour into chilled glasses.
5. Serve and enjoy an immediate energy kick!

NUTRITIONAL VALUES: Packed with Vitamin C, A, and anti-inflammatory properties.

RADIANT RASPBERRY RALLY

P.T.: 10 minutes
SERVES: 2
INGR:

- 1 cup of raspberries
- 2 kiwis, peeled
- 1/2 cup of pineapple chunks
- A handful of mint leaves
- 1 tablespoon of chia seeds

PROCEDURE:

1. Prepare all the fresh ingredients.
2. Juice raspberries, kiwis, pineapple, and mint leaves.
3. Pour into serving glasses.
4. Sprinkle chia seeds on top.
5. Stir slightly and enjoy.

NUTRITIONAL VALUES: High in Vitamin C, E, antioxidants, and dietary fiber.

ELECTRIC ELDERBERRY ENERGIZER

P.T.: 12 minutes
SERVES: 2
INGR:

- 1 cup of elderberries
- 1 banana
- 1/2 cup of Greek yogurt
- 1 tablespoon of flaxseeds
- A sprinkle of cinnamon

PROCEDURE:

1. Prepare and wash elderberries.
2. In a blender, blend elderberries, banana, and Greek yogurt.
3. Pour the smooth blend into glasses.
4. Top with flaxseeds and a sprinkle of cinnamon.
5. Stir gently and savor the zest.

NUTRITIONAL VALUES: High in antioxidants, omega-3 fatty acids, and probiotics.

VIVACIOUS VANILLA VITALIZER

P.T.: 8 minutes
SERVES: 2
INGR:

- 1 cup of almond milk
- 1 teaspoon of vanilla extract
- 1 date, pitted
- 1 tablespoon of cocoa powder
- 1/2 an avocado

PROCEDURE:

1. In a blender, combine all ingredients.
2. Blend until smooth and creamy.
3. Pour the mixture into glasses.
4. Garnish with a sprinkle of cocoa powder.
5. Enjoy the creamy delight.

NUTRITIONAL VALUES: Loaded with healthy fats, fibers, and magnesium.

NECTAROUS NUTMEG NUDGE

P.T.: 7 minutes
SERVES: 2
INGR:

- 1 cup of coconut water
- A pinch of nutmeg
- 1/2 a mango, peeled
- 1/2 teaspoon of spirulina powder
- A drizzle of agave syrup

PROCEDURE:

1. Blend coconut water, mango, and spirulina in a blender.
2. Pour into glasses.
3. Drizzle with agave syrup.
4. Sprinkle nutmeg on top.
5. Stir and relish the tropical charm.

NUTRITIONAL VALUES: Rich in electrolytes, Vitamin A, and detoxifying agents.

PEPPERY PEACH PUMP

P.T.: 8 minutes
SERVES: 2
INGR:

- 2 peaches, pitted
- 1/2 a lemon, peeled
- A pinch of black pepper
- 1 teaspoon of goji berries
- A splash of almond milk

PROCEDURE:

1. Prepare and wash the peaches and lemon.
2. Juice peaches and lemon together.
3. Add a splash of almond milk and stir.
4. Pour into glasses and top with goji berries.
5. Sprinkle black pepper for an added kick.

NUTRITIONAL VALUES: High in Vitamin C, E, and antioxidants.

BLISSFUL BANANA BREEZE

P.T.: 6 minutes
SERVES: 2
INGR:

- 2 bananas
- 1/2 cup of oat milk
- 1/2 a teaspoon of maca powder
- 1 tablespoon of honey
- A sprinkle of sea salt

PROCEDURE:

1. Blend bananas, oat milk, and maca powder until smooth.
2. Drizzle in honey and blend again.
3. Pour the creamy mixture into glasses.
4. Sprinkle a pinch of sea salt on top.
5. Sip and enjoy the comforting blend.

NUTRITIONAL VALUES: High in potassium, fibers, and mood-enhancing properties.

VIVID VEGGIE VIGOR

P.T.: 9 minutes
SERVES: 2
INGR:

- 1 carrot
- 1 beetroot
- 1 celery stalk
- A handful of kale
- 1/2 a cucumber

PROCEDURE:

1. Wash and prepare all vegetables.
2. Juice carrot, beetroot, celery, kale, and cucumber.
3. Pour the vibrant blend into glasses.
4. Stir and enjoy the earthy goodness.
5. Best consumed immediately for maximum benefits.

NUTRITIONAL VALUES: Loaded with minerals. Vitamin A, K, C, and essential

CHERRY CHARGE CHALLENGE

P.T.: 8 minutes
SERVES: 2
INGR:

- 1 cup of cherries, pitted
- 1/2 an apple
- A thumb of ginger
- A splash of coconut water
- 1 teaspoon of acai powder

PROCEDURE:

1. Prepare the cherries and apple.
2. Juice cherries, apple, and ginger.
3. Pour into glasses and add a splash of coconut water.
4. Stir in acai powder.
5. Enjoy the sweet and spicy energy lift.

NUTRITIONAL VALUES: High in antioxidants, Vitamin C, and energy-boosting compounds.

ELECTRIC ESPRESSO ESCAPE

P.T.: 7 minutes
SERVES: 2
INGR:

- 1 shot of espresso (cooled)
- 1 banana
- 1 teaspoon of cacao nibs
- 1/2 cup of almond milk
- A touch of vanilla extract

PROCEDURE:

1. Combine cooled espresso, banana, almond milk, and vanilla extract in a blender.
2. Blend until smooth.
3. Pour into serving glasses.
4. Sprinkle cacao nibs on top.
5. Savor the creamy caffeinated boost.

NUTRITIONAL VALUES: Rich in potassium, magnesium, and a caffeine kick.

INVIGORATING IVORY INSIGHT

P.T.: 6 minutes
SERVES: 2
INGR:

- 1 cup of coconut milk
- 1 teaspoon of honey
- A hint of cinnamon
- 1 teaspoon of chia seeds
- 1/2 a papaya, deseeded

PROCEDURE:

1. Blend coconut milk, honey, cinnamon, and papaya until creamy.
2. Pour into glasses.
3. Sprinkle with chia seeds.
4. Stir slightly and relish.
5. Best consumed chilled.

NUTRITIONAL VALUES: High in fiber, Vitamin C, and healthy fats.

BOLD BLACKBERRY BLITZ

P.T.: 8 minutes
SERVES: 2
INGR:

- 1 cup of blackberries
- 1/2 a lime, peeled
- 1 tablespoon of agave nectar
- A thumb of ginger
- 1/2 cup of water

PROCEDURE:

1. Wash and prepare the blackberries and lime.
2. Juice blackberries, lime, and ginger.
3. Pour into glasses.
4. Sweeten with agave nectar.
5. Stir and enjoy the tangy zing.

NUTRITIONAL VALUES: Rich in Vitamin C, fiber, and metabolism-enhancing properties.

PERKY PASSION PUNCH

P.T.: 9 minutes
SERVES: 2
INGR:

- 1 passion fruit, halved and scooped
- 1 orange, peeled
- 1/2 a lemon, peeled
- A pinch of sea salt
- A splash of sparkling water

PROCEDURE:

1. Juice the passion fruit, orange, and lemon.
2. Pour into glasses.
3. Add a pinch of sea salt.
4. Top off with sparkling water.
5. Gently stir and relish the effervescent boost.

NUTRITIONAL VALUES: High in Vitamin A, C, and revitalizing electrolytes.

VITAL VINEGAR VIBE

P.T.: 5 minutes
SERVES: 2
INGR:

- 1 tablespoon of apple cider vinegar
- 1 apple
- A hint of cayenne pepper
- 1 teaspoon of honey
- 1/2 cup of water

PROCEDURE:

1. Juice the apple.
2. Combine apple juice, apple cider vinegar, and water in a jug.
3. Sweeten with honey.
4. Pour into glasses and sprinkle cayenne pepper.
5. Stir and consume for an energized day ahead.

NUTRITIONAL VALUES: Rich in digestive enzymes, metabolism boosters, and Vitamin C.

JUBILANT JICAMA JOLT

P.T.: 8 minutes
SERVES: 2
INGR:

- 1 jicama, peeled and chopped
- 1/2 a grapefruit, peeled
- A hint of pink Himalayan salt
- 1 teaspoon of lemon zest
- 1/2 cup of coconut water

PROCEDURE:

1. Juice jicama and grapefruit.
2. Pour into glasses.
3. Add coconut water.
4. Sprinkle with pink salt and lemon zest.
5. Enjoy the crisp and invigorating boost.

NUTRITIONAL VALUES: High in Vitamin C, E, and essential minerals.

TITILLATING TURMERIC TONIC

P.T.: 7 minutes
SERVES: 2
INGR:

- A thumb-sized piece of turmeric
- 1 cup of carrot juice
- A pinch of black pepper
- 1 teaspoon of olive oil
- A touch of lemon juice

PROCEDURE:

1. Juice turmeric and mix with fresh carrot juice.
2. Pour into glasses.
3. Add olive oil and a touch of lemon juice.
4. Sprinkle with black pepper to enhance turmeric absorption.
5. Stir well and savor the vibrant boost.

NUTRITIONAL VALUES: Rich in anti-inflammatory properties, Vitamin A, and healthy fats.

FIERY FIG FERVOR

P.T.: 9 minutes
SERVES: 2
INGR:

- 2 fresh figs, quartered
- 1 cup of almond milk
- 1/2 a teaspoon of cinnamon
- A pinch of nutmeg
- 1 teaspoon of maple syrup

PROCEDURE:

1. Blend figs, almond milk, and spices until creamy.
2. Pour into glasses.
3. Sweeten with maple syrup.
4. Stir and cherish the velvety energy surge.
5. Best consumed immediately for a delightful lift.

NUTRITIONAL VALUES: High in calcium, fiber, and essential minerals.

JAZZY JAVA JIVE

P.T.: 6 minutes
SERVES: 2
INGR:

- 1 shot of cold espresso
- 1/2 a cup of oat milk
- 1 teaspoon of cocoa powder
- A touch of vanilla extract
- A dash of cinnamon

PROCEDURE:

1. Combine espresso, oat milk, cocoa, and vanilla in a blender.
2. Blend until smooth and frothy.
3. Pour into glasses.
4. Sprinkle with cinnamon.
5. Enjoy the energizing coffee embrace.

NUTRITIONAL VALUES: High in antioxidants, magnesium, and a delightful caffeine buzz.

Juices for Specific Health Concerns (Digestion, Immunity, Skin Health)

DIGESTIVE DELIGHT

P.T.: 7 minutes
SERVES: 1
INGR.:

- 1 fennel bulb
- 2 green apples
- 1-inch piece of ginger
- A handful of mint leaves
- 1/2 cucumber

PROCEDURE:

1. Begin by juicing the fennel bulb and green apples.
2. Add in the ginger and mint leaves.
3. Finish with the cucumber for a cooling sensation.
4. Stir everything and serve chilled.
5. Consume before meals for best results.

NUTRITIONAL VALUES: 105 calories, 0.5g fat, 26g carbs, 1.5g protein, 6g fiber, 18g sugar.

IMMUNE BOOSTER

P.T.: 5 minutes
SERVES: 1
INGR.:

- 3 oranges, peeled
- 1-inch piece of turmeric
- 1-inch piece of ginger
- A pinch of black pepper
- 1 carrot

PROCEDURE:

1. Juice the oranges for a vitamin C boost.
2. Add the turmeric, ginger, and carrot.
3. Finish with a sprinkle of black pepper to enhance turmeric absorption.
4. Stir well and serve.
5. Best taken in the morning for an immunity surge.

NUTRITIONAL VALUES: 130 calories, 0.7g fat, 31g carbs, 2g protein, 7g fiber, 21g sugar.

SKIN RENEWAL

P.T.: 8 minutes
SERVES: 1
INGR.:

- 1 cucumber
- 2 celery stalks
- 1/2 beetroot
- 2 kiwis, peeled
- A handful of spinach

PROCEDURE:

1. Begin with the cucumber and celery for hydration.
2. Add beetroot for detoxification.

3. Incorporate kiwi for its vitamin C and antioxidants.
4. Finish with spinach for its rich vitamins and minerals.
5. Mix well and serve. Consume regularly for a natural glow.

NUTRITIONAL VALUES: 120 calories, 0.6g fat, 28g carbs, 2.2g protein, 8g fiber, 17g sugar.

GUT RELIEF

P.T.: 6 minutes
SERVES: 1
INGR.:

- 1 papaya, peeled
- 1/2 banana
- A handful of parsley
- 1-inch piece of ginger
- 1/4 pineapple

PROCEDURE:

1. Juice the papaya, renowned for its digestive enzymes.
2. Add banana for its gut-friendly fiber.
3. Incorporate parsley for detoxification.
4. Add ginger for its calming properties.
5. Finish with pineapple and serve. Best taken post meals.

NUTRITIONAL VALUES: 110 calories, 0.4g fat, 27g carbs, 1.8g protein, 5g fiber, 20g sugar.

ALLERGY ALLEVIATOR

P.T.: 5 minutes
SERVES: 1
INGR.:

- 3 apples
- 1-inch piece of ginger
- A handful of nettles
- 1/4 lemon
- 2 celery stalks

PROCEDURE:

1. Juice the apples and celery.
2. Incorporate ginger for its anti-inflammatory properties.
3. Add nettles, known to alleviate allergy symptoms.
4. Finish with a squeeze of lemon for a tang. Serve immediately.

NUTRITIONAL VALUES: 125 calories, 0.5g fat, 30g carbs, 1.5g protein, 6g fiber, 22g sugar.

HEARTY HEART

P.T.: 6 minutes
SERVES: 1
INGR.:

- 3 tomatoes
- A handful of basil
- 1/2 red bell pepper
- 1 garlic clove
- 1/4 lemon

PROCEDURE:

1. Begin with juicing tomatoes.
2. Add red bell pepper for its antioxidants.
3. Incorporate basil for its heart-friendly benefits.
4. Add a garlic clove for its cholesterol-lowering properties.
5. Finish with lemon and serve.

NUTRITIONAL VALUES: 90 calories, 0.3g fat, 21g carbs, 1.2g protein, 4g fiber, 15g sugar.

BONE BUILDER

P.T.: 7 minutes
SERVES: 1
INGR.:

- 1 cup of kale
- 1 green apple
- 1/2 orange, peeled
- 1/2 kiwi
- 2 broccoli florets

PROCEDURE:

1. Juice the kale and green apple.
2. Incorporate orange for its vitamin C.
3. Add kiwi for additional vitamins.
4. Finish with broccoli, known for its bone-building properties.
5. Stir and serve chilled.

NUTRITIONAL VALUES: 95 calories, 0.4g fat, 22g carbs, 1.4g protein, 5g fiber, 16g sugar.

LIVER LOVER

P.T.: 8 minutes
SERVES: 1
INGR.:

- 1/2 beetroot
- 1 carrot
- 1 green apple
- 1-inch piece of turmeric
- A handful of dandelion greens

PROCEDURE:

1. Start by juicing beetroot, known for liver detox.
2. Add carrot and green apple.
3. Incorporate turmeric for its anti-inflammatory benefits.
4. Finish with dandelion greens, great for liver health. Serve immediately.

NUTRITIONAL VALUES: 105 calories, 0.5g fat, 24g carbs, 1.5g protein, 6g fiber, 18g sugar.

BRAIN BOOST

P.T.: 6 minutes
SERVES: 1
INGR.:

- 1/4 cabbage
- 1 blueberry handful
- 1/2 avocado, peeled
- 1/2 lemon
- 1 spinach handful

PROCEDURE:

1. Juice the cabbage, known for its brain-boosting properties.
2. Incorporate blueberries, rich in antioxidants.
3. Add avocado for its beneficial fats.
4. Squeeze in lemon for a zesty twist.
5. Finish with spinach and serve chilled.

NUTRITIONAL VALUES: 115 calories, 0.6g fat, 27g carbs, 1.6g protein, 7g fiber, 19g sugar.

LUNG LIFTER

P.T.: 7 minutes
SERVES: 1
INGR.:

- 2 pears
- 1/4 pineapple
- A handful of watercress
- 1/2 lemon
- 1-inch piece of ginger

PROCEDURE:

1. Juice pears and pineapple for sweetness.
2. Add watercress, beneficial for lungs.
3. Incorporate ginger for its respiratory benefits.

4. Finish with lemon and serve fresh.

NUTRITIONAL VALUES: 110 calories, 0.4g fat, 26g carbs, 1.5g protein, 6g fiber, 20g sugar.

INFLAMMATION TAMER

P.T.: 5 minutes
SERVES: 1
INGR.:

- 2 celery stalks
- 1 cucumber
- 1-inch piece of turmeric
- 1/2 lemon
- A handful of pineapple chunks

PROCEDURE:

1. Begin by juicing the celery stalks and cucumber.
2. Incorporate turmeric, known for its anti-inflammatory properties.
3. Add the pineapple chunks for sweetness and added enzymes.
4. Finish with a squeeze of lemon for a refreshing twist.
5. Serve immediately for best taste.

NUTRITIONAL VALUES: 95 calories, 0.3g fat, 23g carbs, 1.2g protein, 5g fiber, 17g sugar.

DIGESTIVE DYNAMO

P.T.: 5 minutes
SERVES: 2
INGR:

- 1 medium fennel bulb
- 1 apple
- 1 thumb-sized ginger piece
- A touch of mint leaves
- 1/2 cup of water

PROCEDURE:

1. Wash and chop fennel, apple, and ginger.
2. Juice them along with mint leaves.
3. Pour into glasses.
4. Stir gently and serve.
5. Best consumed before meals for optimal digestive support.

NUTRITIONAL VALUES: High in dietary fiber, vitamin C, and aids digestion.

IMMUNITY INFUSION

P.T.: 6 minutes
SERVES: 2
INGR:

- 2 oranges
- 1/2 grapefruit
- A thumb-sized turmeric piece
- A pinch of black pepper
- 1/2 cup of water

PROCEDURE:

1. Peel and prepare oranges and grapefruit.
2. Juice them with turmeric.
3. Pour into glasses.
4. Add a pinch of black pepper to enhance absorption.
5. Stir gently and consume immediately.

NUTRITIONAL VALUES: Rich in vitamin C, anti-inflammatory properties, and boosts immunity.

SKIN SPARKLER

P.T.: 7 minutes
SERVES: 2
INGR:

- 1 cucumber
- 2 carrots
- A hint of parsley
- 1/2 beetroot
- 1/2 cup of water

PROCEDURE:

1. Prepare and chop cucumber, carrots, and beetroot.
2. Juice them along with parsley.
3. Pour into glasses.
4. Stir well and serve chilled.
5. Drink regularly for radiant skin.

NUTRITIONAL VALUES: High in vitamin A, antioxidants, and promotes skin health.

GUT GLORY

P.T.: 6 minutes

SERVES: 2

INGR:

- 1 papaya, deseeded
- 1 thumb-sized ginger piece
- 1/2 a lemon
- A touch of honey
- 1/2 cup of water

PROCEDURE:

1. Prepare papaya and juice it with ginger and lemon.
2. Pour into glasses.
3. Sweeten with honey.
4. Stir well and relish.
5. Consume regularly for gut health.

NUTRITIONAL VALUES: Rich in digestive enzymes, vitamin C, and aids in gut health.

ALLERGEN ASSASSIN

P.T.: 6 minutes

SERVES: 2

INGR:

- 1 apple
- 1 celery stalk
- 1/4 pineapple
- A hint of nettle leaves
- 1/2 cup of water

PROCEDURE:

1. Prepare apple, celery, and pineapple.
2. Juice them with nettle leaves.
3. Pour into glasses.
4. Stir gently and serve.
5. Drink regularly for allergen resistance.

NUTRITIONAL VALUES: High in vitamin C, bromelain, and anti-allergenic properties.

CARDIAC CARETAKER

P.T.: 7 minutes

SERVES: 2

INGR:

- 2 tomatoes
- 1/2 a red bell pepper
- A hint of basil leaves
- A touch of black salt
- 1/2 cup of water

PROCEDURE:

1. Prepare tomatoes and bell pepper.
2. Juice them along with basil leaves.
3. Pour into glasses.
4. Add black salt for taste.
5. Stir well and savor the heart-healthy drink.

NUTRITIONAL VALUES: Rich in lycopene, vitamin C, and promotes heart health.

BONE BENEFACTOR

P.T.: 6 minutes
SERVES: 2
INGR:

- 2 cups of spinach
- 1 orange
- 1 kiwi
- A hint of sesame seeds
- 1/2 cup of water

PROCEDURE:

1. Wash spinach thoroughly.
2. Peel orange and kiwi.
3. Juice spinach, orange, and kiwi.
4. Pour into glasses.
5. Sprinkle sesame seeds on top before serving.

NUTRITIONAL VALUES: High in calcium, vitamin K, and strengthens bones.

LIVER LUMINARY

P.T.: 6 minutes
SERVES: 2
INGR:

- 2 beetroots
- 1 carrot
- A thumb-sized turmeric piece
- A hint of cilantro
- 1/2 cup of water

PROCEDURE:

1. Prepare and chop beetroots and carrot.
2. Juice them with turmeric and cilantro.
3. Pour into glasses.
4. Stir well and consume.
5. Drink periodically for liver wellness.

NUTRITIONAL VALUES: Rich in antioxidants, anti-inflammatory properties, and aids liver detoxification.

BRAIN BREEZE

P.T.: 7 minutes
SERVES: 2
INGR:

- 1 cup of blueberries
- 1/2 an avocado
- A hint of walnuts
- A touch of honey
- 1/2 cup of water

PROCEDURE:

1. Prepare blueberries and avocado.
2. Blend them with walnuts and water.
3. Pour into glasses.
4. Sweeten with honey.
5. Drink for a mental boost.

NUTRITIONAL VALUES: Rich in omega-3 fatty acids, antioxidants, and promotes brain health.

LUNG LEVITATOR

P.T.: 6 minutes
SERVES: 2
INGR:

- 1 cup of kale
- 1 apple
- 1/4 pineapple
- A hint of thyme
- 1/2 cup of water

PROCEDURE:

1. Wash kale thoroughly.
2. Prepare apple and pineapple.
3. Juice kale, apple, pineapple, and thyme.
4. Pour into glasses.
5. Drink for lung wellness.

NUTRITIONAL VALUES: High in vitamin K, C, and promotes lung health.

INFLAMMATION INSURGENT

P.T.: 7 minutes
SERVES: 2
INGR:

- 1/2 a pineapple
- A thumb-sized ginger piece
- A hint of rosemary
- 1 orange
- 1/2 cup of water

PROCEDURE:

1. Prepare pineapple and orange.
2. Juice them with ginger and rosemary.
3. Pour into glasses.
4. Stir well and enjoy the refreshing flavor.
5. Consume regularly for its anti-inflammatory properties.

NUTRITIONAL VALUES: Rich in bromelain, vitamin C, and fights inflammation.

SINUS SOOTHER

P.T.: 5 minutes
SERVES: 2
INGR:

- 1/2 lemon
- 1 thumb-sized ginger piece
- 1 apple
- A hint of cayenne pepper
- 1/2 cup of water

PROCEDURE:

1. Squeeze lemon juice and prepare the apple.
2. Juice apple with ginger.
3. Pour into glasses.
4. Add a pinch of cayenne pepper.
5. Stir well and drink to help clear sinuses.

NUTRITIONAL VALUES: Rich in vitamin C, anti-inflammatory properties, and helps with sinus congestion.

MOOD MODULATOR

P.T.: 6 minutes
SERVES: 2
INGR:

- 1 banana
- 1/2 cup of spinach
- 1/2 a lemon
- A touch of honey
- 1/2 cup of water

PROCEDURE:

1. Blend banana with spinach and water.
2. Squeeze in lemon juice.
3. Pour into glasses.
4. Sweeten with honey.
5. Drink to uplift mood.

NUTRITIONAL VALUES: High in potassium, magnesium, and promotes serotonin production.

ARTHRITIS ALLEVIATOR

P.T.: 7 minutes
SERVES: 2
INGR:

- 2 carrots
- 1 celery stalk
- 1 thumb-sized turmeric piece
- A pinch of black pepper
- 1/2 cup of water

PROCEDURE:

1. Prepare and chop carrots and celery.
2. Juice them with turmeric.
3. Pour into glasses.
4. Add black pepper for absorption.
5. Drink regularly to alleviate arthritis symptoms.

NUTRITIONAL VALUES: Rich in anti-inflammatory properties and vitamin K.

HORMONE HARMONIZER

P.T.: 6 minutes
SERVES: 2
INGR:

- 1/2 cup of broccoli sprouts
- 1 apple
- A touch of flaxseeds
- 1/4 beetroot
- 1/2 cup of water

PROCEDURE:

1. Prepare apple and beetroot.
2. Juice them with broccoli sprouts.
3. Pour into glasses.
4. Sprinkle flaxseeds on top.
5. Consume for hormonal balance.

NUTRITIONAL VALUES: Rich in sulforaphane, lignans, and promotes hormonal balance.

KIDNEY CLEANSER

P.T.: 5 minutes
SERVES: 2
INGR:

- 1/2 watermelon (without seeds)
- 1 cucumber
- A hint of parsley
- A pinch of Himalayan salt
- 1/2 cup of water

PROCEDURE:

1. Prepare watermelon and cucumber.
2. Juice them with parsley.
3. Pour into glasses.
4. Add a pinch of Himalayan salt.
5. Drink for kidney health.

NUTRITIONAL VALUES: High in hydration, diuretic properties, and supports kidney function.

BLOOD PRESSURE BALANCER

P.T.: 6 minutes

SERVES: 2

INGR:

- 2 celery stalks
- 1 beetroot
- 1/2 lemon
- A touch of chia seeds
- 1/2 cup of water

PROCEDURE:

1. Prepare and chop celery and beetroot.
2. Juice them with lemon.
3. Pour into glasses.
4. Sprinkle with chia seeds.
5. Consume for blood pressure regulation.

NUTRITIONAL VALUES: Rich in nitrates, potassium, and promotes cardiovascular health.

VISION VITALIZER

P.T.: 5 minutes

SERVES: 2

INGR:

- 2 carrots
- 1/2 cup of blueberries
- A touch of goji berries
- A hint of spinach
- 1/2 cup of water

PROCEDURE:

1. Prepare and chop carrots.
2. Juice carrots with spinach.
3. Add blueberries and goji berries to the mix.
4. Blend till smooth.
5. Pour and drink for eye health.

NUTRITIONAL VALUES: High in vitamin A, antioxidants, and supports eye health.

METABOLISM MAVEN

P.T.: 5 minutes

SERVES: 2

INGR:

- 1/2 grapefruit
- 1/4 pineapple
- A pinch of cayenne pepper
- A touch of honey
- 1/2 cup of water

PROCEDURE:

1. Prepare grapefruit and pineapple.
2. Juice both fruits.
3. Pour into glasses.
4. Add cayenne pepper and honey.
5. Drink to boost metabolism.

NUTRITIONAL VALUES: Rich in vitamin C, bromelain, and stimulates metabolism.

STRESS SUBLIMATOR

P.T.: 6 minutes
SERVES: 2
INGR:

- 1/2 cup of chamomile flowers
- 1 apple
- 1/2 lemon
- A touch of honey
- 1/2 cup of water

PROCEDURE:

1. Prepare and chop apple.
2. Juice apple with chamomile flowers.
3. Squeeze in lemon juice.
4. Pour into glasses.
5. Sweeten with honey and drink for relaxation.

NUTRITIONAL VALUES: Rich in antioxidants, calming properties, and aids in stress relief.

THYROID THRIVER

P.T.: 7 minutes
SERVES: 2
INGR:

- 1/2 cup of seaweed (like kelp)
- 1 cucumber
- 1 apple
- A pinch of Himalayan salt
- 1/2 cup of water

PROCEDURE:

1. Prepare apple and cucumber.
2. Juice them with seaweed.
3. Pour into glasses.
4. Add a pinch of Himalayan salt.
5. Consume for thyroid support.

NUTRITIONAL VALUES: High in iodine, hydration, and promotes thyroid health.

SUGAR STABILIZER

P.T.: 5 minutes
SERVES: 2
INGR:

- 1 cinnamon stick
- 1 apple
- A hint of fenugreek seeds
- 1/4 lemon
- 1/2 cup of water

PROCEDURE:

1. Juice apple and lemon together.
2. Add water and cinnamon stick to the blender.
3. Blend with fenugreek seeds till smooth.
4. Pour into glasses.
5. Consume for stable blood sugar levels.

NUTRITIONAL VALUES: Helps with insulin sensitivity, antioxidant-rich, and supports healthy glucose levels.

JOINT JUBILEE

P.T.: 5 minutes
SERVES: 2
INGR:

- 2 carrots
- 1/2 pineapple
- 1 thumb-sized turmeric piece
- A pinch of black pepper
- 1/2 cup of water

PROCEDURE:

1. Prepare and chop carrots and pineapple.
2. Juice them with turmeric.
3. Pour into glasses.
4. Add black pepper for absorption.
5. Consume to support joint health.

NUTRITIONAL VALUES: High in anti-inflammatory agents, bromelain, and aids joint health.

MUSCLE MAINTAINER

P.T.: 6 minutes
SERVES: 2
INGR:

- 1 banana
- 1/4 cup of spinach
- 1 tablespoon of almond butter
- A hint of chia seeds
- 1/2 cup of water

PROCEDURE:

1. Blend banana, spinach, and almond butter.
2. Pour into glasses.
3. Top with chia seeds.
4. Mix well before consuming.
5. Drink to support muscle health.

NUTRITIONAL VALUES: Rich in potassium, magnesium, and protein for muscle health.

NERVE NOURISHER

P.T.: 5 minutes
SERVES: 2
INGR:

- 2 celery stalks
- 1 apple
- 1/2 avocado
- A pinch of Himalayan salt
- 1/2 cup of water

PROCEDURE:

1. Prepare and chop celery and apple.
2. Juice them, then blend with avocado.
3. Pour into glasses.
4. Add a pinch of Himalayan salt.
5. Consume for nerve function support.

NUTRITIONAL VALUES: High in essential fats, sodium, and supports nerve health.

ANTI-AGING AMBROSIA

P.T.: 6 minutes
SERVES: 2
INGR:

- 1/4 cup of blueberries
- 1/2 pomegranate
- 1/4 beetroot
- A touch of flaxseeds
- 1/2 cup of water

PROCEDURE:

1. Prepare pomegranate and beetroot.
2. Juice them with blueberries.
3. Pour into glasses.
4. Sprinkle with flaxseeds.
5. Drink for youthful skin and anti-aging benefits.

NUTRITIONAL VALUES: Rich in antioxidants, vitamin C, and promotes skin health.

MIGRAINE MITIGATOR

P.T.: 5 minutes
SERVES: 2
INGR:

- 1/2 cucumber
- 1/2 lemon
- A hint of ginger
- A pinch of Himalayan salt
- 1/2 cup of water

PROCEDURE:

1. Juice cucumber with ginger.
2. Squeeze in lemon juice.
3. Pour into glasses.
4. Add a pinch of salt.
5. Consume at the onset of migraine symptoms.

NUTRITIONAL VALUES: Hydrating, anti-inflammatory, and aids in reducing migraine intensity.

FATIGUE FIGHTER

P.T.: 7 minutes
SERVES: 2
INGR:

- 1/2 orange
- 1/4 cup of spinach
- 1/4 cup of strawberries
- 1 tablespoon of honey
- 1/2 cup of water

PROCEDURE:

1. Juice orange with strawberries.
2. Blend with spinach and water.
3. Pour into glasses.
4. Sweeten with honey.
5. Drink for an energy boost.

NUTRITIONAL VALUES: Rich in vitamin C, iron, and aids in combating fatigue.

INSOMNIA INHIBITOR

P.T.: 5 minutes
SERVES: 2
INGR:

- 1/2 cup of cherry juice
- 1/2 banana
- A hint of nutmeg
- 1 tablespoon of honey
- 1/2 cup of water

PROCEDURE:

1. Blend banana with cherry juice.
2. Add water and blend smoothly.
3. Pour into glasses.
4. Add a touch of nutmeg and honey.
5. Drink before bed for better sleep.

NUTRITIONAL VALUES: Rich in melatonin, magnesium, and promotes sleep.

HAIR HERO

P.T.: 6 minutes
SERVES: 2
INGR:

- 2 carrots
- 1/2 cucumber
- 1/4 avocado
- A hint of flaxseed oil
- 1/2 cup of water

PROCEDURE:

1. Juice carrots and cucumber.
2. Blend with avocado and water.
3. Pour into glasses.
4. Mix in flaxseed oil.
5. Consume for hair nourishment.

NUTRITIONAL VALUES: Rich in biotin, vitamin E, and promotes hair health.

STAMINA STRENGTHENER

P.T.: 7 minutes
SERVES: 2
INGR:

- 1/2 beetroot
- 1/4 pineapple
- A touch of maca powder
- 1 tablespoon of honey
- 1/2 cup of water

PROCEDURE:

1. Juice beetroot and pineapple.
2. Pour into glasses.
3. Add maca powder and honey.
4. Stir well.
5. Drink to enhance stamina.

NUTRITIONAL VALUES: High in nitrates, bromelain, and boosts endurance.

LYMPHATIC LUXE

P.T.: 6 minutes
SERVES: 2
INGR:

- 1/2 lemon
- 2 celery stalks
- A hint of parsley
- 1 tablespoon of honey
- 1/2 cup of water

PROCEDURE:

1. Juice lemon and celery stalks.
2. Add parsley and blend.
3. Pour into glasses.
4. Sweeten with honey.
5. Consume for lymphatic health.

NUTRITIONAL VALUES: Rich in vitamin C, chlorophyll, and promotes lymphatic drainage.

ADRENAL AID

P.T.: 5 minutes
SERVES: 2
INGR:

- 1/4 apple
- 1/2 banana
- A hint of ashwagandha powder
- 1 tablespoon of honey
- 1/2 cup of water

PROCEDURE:

1. Blend apple and banana together.
2. Pour into glasses.
3. Add ashwagandha powder and honey.
4. Stir well.
5. Drink to support adrenal health.

NUTRITIONAL VALUES: High in adaptogens, natural sugars, and supports adrenal function.

Chapter 7: Challenges & Solutions

Overcoming Common Juicing Mistakes

Juicing has become a mainstream health phenomenon, with many people diving into this nutritious world in search of wellness. But as with any culinary adventure, it has its pitfalls. As they say, "To err is human." But fret not, dear reader, because understanding and avoiding these pitfalls will ensure that your juicing journey is both enjoyable and beneficial.

The Enigma of the Bitter Aftertaste
Imagine this: you've just juiced your favorite fruits and veggies, but the end result has a strange bitterness. This unexpected taste might be due to the inclusion of fruit seeds, especially from apples or grapes. These seeds can often introduce a slightly bitter flavor. To overcome this, always ensure you deseed fruits where possible or choose seedless varieties.

The Overzealous Green Juice
We've all been there. In an attempt to maximize health benefits, we end up adding all the green veggies we can find. The end result? A glass that tastes more like a meadow than a refreshing drink. Balance is key in juicing. Mixing potent greens like kale or wheatgrass with sweeter fruits like apples or pineapples can help neutralize overpowering flavors, making your green juice palatable and still packed with nutrients.

The Fading Color Conundrum
Drinking a gray or brown juice can be a less than appetizing experience, even if it tastes fantastic. This discoloration often results when fruits and vegetables oxidize. To combat this, add a splash of lemon juice to your concoction. Not only will it preserve the vibrant colors, but it will also add a zesty punch to your drink.

Forgetting the Pulp
Many juicing aficionados make the rookie mistake of discarding the pulp. This fibrous byproduct is filled with nutrients and can be incorporated into soups, stews, or even used as a base for vegetable broth. By utilizing the pulp, you're maximizing the nutritional value of your produce and minimizing waste.

Addressing Nutritional Concerns (e.g., Sugar Intake)

Juicing offers a concentrated dose of vitamins, minerals, and other beneficial compounds. However, it also presents a unique set of challenges, particularly when it comes to sugar. How do we maximize the nutritional benefits of juicing while minimizing potential drawbacks?

The Sugary Slip-Up
Juices, especially those primarily made from fruits, can be high in natural sugars. While these sugars are accompanied by essential nutrients, excessive intake can lead to issues such as weight gain, dental problems, and blood sugar fluctuations. The solution isn't to avoid fruit juices, but to find a harmonious balance.

Veggie to the Rescue
Vegetables are the unsung heroes in the juicing world. Not only do they add a variety of flavors and colors to your glass, but they also balance out the natural sugars from the fruits. For instance, cucumbers, celery, and zucchini have a high water content and a subtle taste, making them perfect for diluting sugar-heavy juices without diluting flavor.

Incorporate Low-Glycemic Fruits
Not all fruits are sugar-bombs. Berries, kiwi, and green apples are examples of fruits that are lower in sugar but rich in flavor. Integrating these fruits can be a game-changer, allowing you to enjoy the sweetness without overwhelming sugar content.

The Power of Moderation
Juicing shouldn't replace whole foods. It's best to think of it as a supplement rather than a primary source of nutrition. One or two glasses a day, preferably combined with a balanced diet, can offer a plethora of health benefits.

Troubleshooting Juicer Issues and Recipe Mishaps

Every passionate juicer has faced it: the moment when the juicer doesn't cooperate or the anticipated flavor of a new recipe goes awry. These moments, while frustrating, are just part of the journey. Let's dive into the common challenges and find ways to ensure they don't halt our juicing enthusiasm.

The Grumbling Juicer
The hum of a juicer is a reassuring sound for many. But what if it starts making a louder noise or, worse, not turning on at all?

1. **Check the Basics**: Sometimes, the solution is as simple as ensuring the juicer is properly assembled. A loose part can prevent the machine from operating.
2. **Clean It Up**: Over time, pulp and other residues can build up and impede the juicer's function. Regular, thorough cleaning can prevent this accumulation from affecting performance.
3. **Stay Cool**: Overheating can be a common issue, especially if you're juicing in large batches. Giving your juicer a short break between sessions can extend its lifespan.

Recipe Regrets

We've all been there. A new juice concoction that sounded promising ends up tasting like a mismatch of flavors.

1. **Balancing Act**: If your juice is too bitter or tangy, add a naturally sweet fruit or vegetable to balance the flavor. Conversely, if it's overly sweet, a touch of lemon or a green vegetable can provide a refreshing counterpoint.
2. **Water It Down**: Sometimes, a splash of cold water or coconut water can dilute an overpowering flavor, making the juice more palatable.
3. **Spice It Right**: If a juice feels bland, consider adding a touch of spices like ginger, turmeric, or even a dash of cayenne pepper for a zesty kick.

Consistency Concerns

There's a fine line between a refreshing juice and an unintended smoothie or a watery drink.

1. **Choose Wisely**: The type of juicer you use can influence the consistency. For instance, masticating juicers typically yield a thicker juice compared to centrifugal ones.
2. **Filter It Out**: If your juice is too pulpy, pouring it through a fine mesh strainer can help you achieve the desired consistency.
3. **Fresh Matters**: The freshness of your produce can also impact the juice's texture. Overripe fruits tend to produce a mushier consistency.

Embracing the world of juicing means accepting occasional mishaps. Yet, with each challenge comes an opportunity to learn and refine. With patience, knowledge, and a touch of creativity, you can turn these hurdles into stepping stones on your path to becoming a master juicer.

Chapter 8: Beyond the Juice - Whole Food Integration

Smoothies vs. Juices: Benefits and Uses

Juicing and smoothie-making are both exceptional practices to incorporate into one's diet, but it's essential to understand their distinct benefits and how each can be optimally used.

The Essence of Juicing

When you juice, you're extracting the liquid from fruits and vegetables, leaving behind the fiber. This gives your body a break from digesting and allows it to absorb nutrients directly. Since fiber is separated, juices offer a concentrated shot of vitamins, minerals, and enzymes, directly entering the bloodstream.

Juices act as a quick energy boost. Think of it as a natural intravenous infusion packed with nutrition, perfect for those mornings when you need an instant pick-me-up or after an intense workout. Plus, since it lacks bulky fiber, it allows for more volume of fruits and vegetables per serving, which means more nutrition in every sip.

The Wholesomeness of Smoothies

On the flip side, smoothies incorporate the whole fruit or vegetable – fiber and all. This fiber plays a pivotal role in digestion. It acts as a slow-releasing source of energy, keeping you full for longer. The presence of fiber also ensures that the natural sugars from the fruits are slowly absorbed, providing steady energy without sharp spikes and crashes.

Smoothies are more than just drinks; they're meals in a glass. You can add proteins, healthy fats, and a myriad of other nutrients. They're perfect for those on-the-go mornings or a midday meal replacement. They can easily be tailored to dietary needs, from muscle-building protein shakes to antioxidant-rich berry blends.

Which One is Right for You?

Neither juices nor smoothies are superior; they serve different purposes. If you're looking for rapid nutrient absorption and an immediate energy boost, go for a juice. But if you're aiming for a fulfilling meal replacement that provides sustained energy, a smoothie is your best bet.

Consider your lifestyle and needs. If you're someone who exercises intensely, a juice might offer that quick replenishment post-workout, while a smoothie could serve as a pre-workout fuel.

Lastly, remember that while both smoothies and juices are beneficial, moderation is key. Over-relying on either can mean missing out on essential nutrients found in other foods. It's all about balance and understanding what your body craves and requires.

In the journey of health and wellness, both juices and smoothies have their place of honor. The key is to harness their unique benefits and seamlessly integrate them into a holistic diet that celebrates both concentrated nutrition and wholesome satiety.

Incorporating Pulp: Reducing Waste and Enhancing Nutrition

In the modern age of sustainability and zero-waste goals, there's a growing focus on utilizing every part of our food. The pulp, the fibrous material left behind after juicing, is often discarded without a second thought. However, this pulp is a hidden gem, rich in nutrients and versatile in its use. By incorporating it into our meals, we not only minimize waste but also introduce an added layer of nutrition and texture to our dishes.

A Treasure Trove of Fiber

The primary component of pulp is dietary fiber, a critical nutrient known for its digestive benefits. It promotes bowel regularity and aids in the prevention of constipation. But its advantages go beyond just aiding digestion.

Fiber can help in managing weight, as it gives a sense of fullness, potentially reducing overall food intake. It also plays a role in regulating blood sugar levels and cholesterol.

Innovative Ways to Use Pulp

The versatility of pulp is astounding. Here are some ways you can reincorporate it into your meals:

- **Baking Boost**: Pulp can be a great addition to baked goods. Whether it's muffins, bread, or pancakes, a bit of fruit or vegetable pulp can enhance moisture and add a subtle, natural sweetness or savory touch.
- **Broths and Soups**: Vegetable pulp can be boiled down into a rich broth, serving as a base for soups or stews. It adds depth, color, and flavor, making your dishes more hearty and robust.

- **Dressings and Sauces**: Pulp can be blended into salad dressings or sauces, thickening them naturally and adding an extra layer of flavor.
- **Natural Thickener**: Instead of using flour or cornstarch, consider using pulp to thicken your dishes. It's especially useful for gravies or creamy dishes, offering a unique texture and nutrient boost.
- **Frozen Treats**: Fruit pulp can be blended with a touch of honey or yogurt and frozen for a delightful, healthy popsicle. It's a refreshing treat, especially during warmer months, and a creative way to get kids to consume more nutrients.

The Environmental Impact

Every bit of food we waste contributes to larger global issues, from increased greenhouse gas emissions to inefficient use of water and land. By finding use for the pulp, we're taking a step toward a more sustainable future. It reflects a deeper respect for our environment and the bounties it offers.

Embracing the pulp is more than just a culinary venture; it's a commitment to health, sustainability, and innovative cooking. It challenges us to look at food differently, to see potential in what was once considered waste, and to craft dishes that are as nutritious as they are delicious.

Complementary Foods for a Balanced Diet

Embarking on a journey of juicing and whole-food integration introduces a plethora of health benefits and tantalizing flavors. However, while juices and smoothies play a significant role in providing essential nutrients, they are just one component of a balanced diet. To ensure optimal health, it's crucial to complement these drinks with other foods that fill in any nutritional gaps and create a well-rounded diet.

The Importance of Protein

Proteins are the building blocks of our body. They support muscle growth, repair tissues, and play a pivotal role in various biochemical processes. While certain fruits and vegetables contain small amounts of protein, they often don't suffice for daily requirements, especially if one is highly active or looking to build muscle.

To complement the nutrients from juices and smoothies, consider incorporating lean proteins like chicken, turkey, fish, or plant-based options such as beans, lentils, and tofu. Not only do these foods support muscle and tissue repair, but they also keep you satiated, ensuring you feel full and energized throughout the day.

Beneficial Fats for Brain and Body

While the term 'fat' might sound daunting to many, certain fats are essential for our well-being.

They aid in absorbing vitamins, provide energy, and support brain health. Avocados, nuts, seeds, olives, and fatty fish like salmon are examples of foods rich in beneficial fats. Including these in your diet ensures that you're feeding your brain and body with what they need to function optimally.

Complex Carbohydrates for Sustained Energy

While juices provide a quick energy boost, complex carbohydrates release energy slowly, ensuring steady blood sugar levels and prolonged vitality. Foods like whole grains, brown rice, quinoa, and starchy vegetables can be excellent additions to meals, offering sustained energy throughout the day.

Diversify with Micronutrients

Beyond macronutrients (protein, fats, and carbohydrates), it's essential to consume a variety of micronutrients, including vitamins and minerals. While juices can provide a substantial amount, diversifying food intake ensures you don't miss out on any crucial elements. Incorporate colorful vegetables, whole grains, lean proteins, and healthy fats to ensure a wide range of micronutrients.

A Symphony of Flavors and Nutrients

A well-balanced diet is akin to a symphony, where each instrument or food group plays its unique role, contributing to a harmonious and holistic health experience. By complementing your juices and smoothies with a variety of other nutrient-rich foods, you're not just consuming nutrients; you're weaving a tapestry of flavors, textures, and health benefits that cater to every cell in your body. This integrative approach ensures that every meal is a step towards a healthier, more vibrant you.

Chapter 9: Building a Juicing Lifestyle

Sourcing Ingredients: Shopping and Growing Your Own

Building a juicing lifestyle is much like painting a masterpiece. The vibrant hues, textures, and tones all stem from the palette you choose. In this case, your palette is the myriad of fruits and vegetables that transform into wholesome, nutritious juices. However, the artistry and flavor begin long before your juicer whirs to life; it starts with how you source your ingredients.

Discovering the Farmer's Bounty

While the aisles of supermarkets are stocked with an array of fruits and vegetables, there's a particular charm and undeniable freshness in local farmers' markets. These bustling hubs aren't just about fresh produce; they are a celebration of seasonality, local farming, and community. By shopping at farmers' markets, you're not only choosing ingredients at their peak freshness but also supporting local businesses and reducing the carbon footprint linked with transporting produce over long distances.

The Joy of Cultivating Green Fingers

Imagine stepping into your backyard or onto your balcony, plucking a ripe tomato still warm from the sun or snipping off a bunch of fresh basil, all ready to be juiced. Growing your own ingredients is not just a sustainable choice but a deeply rewarding one. It forges a connection with the earth, making you an active participant in the journey from soil to sip.

Starting a kitchen garden doesn't require sprawling spaces. Container gardening, vertical gardens, or even indoor hydroponic systems can be the genesis of fresh ingredients for your juices. From zesty lemons to crunchy carrots, when you grow your produce, you're in control. You decide on the type of seeds, the soil, and most importantly, can ensure they are free from harmful pesticides.

Storing Juices: Best Practices for Freshness

When fruits and vegetables are juiced, their protective outer layer is disrupted, exposing the nutrients and enzymes to air. This process, known as oxidation, is the enemy of freshness. It can change the flavor profile, diminish the nutrient content, and give your juice an unappetizing brownish hue.

To combat this, always aim to consume your juice immediately after extraction. But if that's not possible, minimize its contact with air. Pour your juice into a glass bottle or airtight container, leaving minimal space at the top to restrict the amount of oxygen inside. This simple step can greatly reduce the speed of oxidation.

Cooling Matters

The refrigerator is your juice's best friend. Keeping it cold slows down the microbial activity and the degradation of enzymes and vitamins. Always store your juice in the coldest part of your fridge, usually at the back, away from the door. For those in a hurry, placing your juice in the freezer for a short spell can help retain its freshness until you're ready to sip.

Glass Over Plastic

While plastic containers might seem convenient, they can sometimes leach chemicals into your juice. Glass, on the other hand, is non-reactive and doesn't impart any foreign tastes. Opt for dark-colored glass containers if possible, as they can protect the juice from light, another factor that can speed up degradation.

Integrating Juicing into Daily Routines and Social Occasions

Daily Rituals with a Splash of Juice

Morning routines set the tone for the day. For many, this means meditation, a workout, or perhaps a strong cup of coffee. By introducing juicing into this sacred time, you not only nourish your body but also fortify your mind for the day ahead.

Imagine starting your day with a green juice as you sit on your porch, letting the morning sun greet you, or perhaps sipping on a carrot-apple blend post-workout to replenish your energy.

Yet, mornings aren't the only time to integrate juicing. Mid-afternoon, when that familiar lull hits, trade the usual coffee or sugary snack for a refreshing juice. It offers a revitalizing pick-me-up without the inevitable energy crash.

Social Sips and Celebrations

Juicing needn't be a solitary endeavor. In fact, it can be a wonderful way to connect with loved ones. Hosting a brunch? Surprise your guests with a DIY juice bar, offering a variety of fruits, veggies, and a couple of juicers. Not only does it become a delightful activity, but it also sparks conversation and creativity as guests craft their signature blends.

And for those evening gatherings or celebratory moments, consider juice-infused mocktails. A blend of pomegranate, lime, and mint, topped with sparkling water, can be just as festive and sophisticated as any cocktail.

Juicing on the Go

Life is fast-paced. Between meetings, chores, and commitments, finding time for juicing can be tricky. For those bustling days, consider pre-making your juices the night before, storing them as discussed in the previous section. Invest in a quality insulated bottle to keep your juice cool and fresh as you move through your day. That way, you can enjoy a refreshing sip whether you're at the office, running errands, or on a weekend adventure.

Chapter 10: Continuing the Journey

Adapting to Seasonal Changes and Availability

The world around us thrives in cycles. Trees shed their leaves, only to sprout anew when the season shifts. Likewise, as one grows more invested in the juicing lifestyle, it becomes evident that nature's bounty isn't constant but beautifully cyclical. Embracing seasonal changes isn't just about appreciating the world's rhythms; it's also about aligning our diets and our juicing habits with what nature readily provides.

Why Seasonal Juicing Matters

There's a certain magic in sipping a juice that's harmonious with the season. In the sweltering heart of summer, nature provides watermelons, berries, and cucumbers - ingredients that are not just refreshing but also hydrating. Come fall, the earth gifts us apples, pears, and pumpkins, offering flavors that mirror the warmth of the season.

When you juice with the seasons, you aren't just ensuring the freshest flavors; you're also optimizing nutrition. Produce harvested in its prime boasts a richer nutrient profile, a detail that makes a world of difference in juicing.

Navigating the Changing Tides

While the idea of seasonal juicing is romantic, the practicality of it can sometimes be a challenge. After all, one might wonder, "What do I do when my favorite fruit is out of season?"

This is where adaptability becomes key. Say, for instance, you've grown fond of a summer blend of peach and mint. Come winter, peaches are off the table. But could you perhaps substitute it with a winter fruit, like persimmon, which offers its own unique sweetness? It's all about experimenting and discovering new favorites.

Also, remember that while fresh is fantastic, frozen isn't a faux pas. Many fruits, when frozen at their peak, retain much of their nutritional value, offering a way to enjoy them even when they're out of season.

Advanced Juicing Techniques and Recipes

Every journey has its milestones, and as you delve deeper into the world of juicing, you'll find that the basics are just the beginning. Just as a painter starts with primary colors and later dives into the nuances of shades, the avid juicer too can venture beyond the foundational techniques. This chapter illuminates some of those advanced practices and recipes that can elevate your juicing experience.

Cold-Pressed and Proud

The term 'cold-pressed' might sound like a buzzword, but it represents a technique where juice is extracted through hydraulic pressure, ensuring minimal heat and oxidation. The result? A juice that's not just richer in flavor, but one that boasts a more robust nutrient profile. While cold-pressed juicers are an investment, they pay off in the unparalleled quality of juice they produce.

Layering Flavors

Advanced juicing isn't just about equipment; it's also about refining one's palate. Start thinking of your juice as a culinary creation. Experiment with layering flavors, balancing sweet, sour, bitter, and umami. For instance, the sweetness of apple can be beautifully offset by the earthiness of beetroot, rounded off with the tang of lime. Dive into the world of herbs and spices too. A hint of basil or a whisper of cinnamon can completely transform a juice.

The Art of Combinations

While it might be tempting to throw everything into the juicer, restraint can often lead to the most delightful results. Prioritize quality over quantity. An advanced recipe needn't have a plethora of ingredients; sometimes, the magic lies in pairing just two or three components that enhance each other.

Preserving Nutritional Integrity

As you refine your juicing techniques, be mindful of the nutritional aspect. Some nutrients are light-sensitive, some are water-soluble.

Educate yourself on these nuances. For instance, using a dark, airtight container can prolong the life of certain nutrients in your juice.

Expanding Your Palate: Exploring Global Juicing Traditions

The Indian Ayurvedic Approach

India, with its ancient Ayurvedic traditions, has long revered the power of nature's produce.

Here, juices aren't just beverages; they're medicine. Consider the 'Tulsi Kadha,' a warm blend of holy basil, black pepper, and honey. It's not only a soothing drink but is also believed to boost immunity. Or the 'Amla Juice,' made from the Indian gooseberry, celebrated for its rejuvenating properties and a rich source of Vitamin C.

Mexico's Traditional 'Aguas Frescas'

Journey to the heart of Mexico, and you'll encounter 'Aguas Frescas,' refreshing beverages made from fruits blended with water and a touch of sweetener. Popular flavors include 'Agua de Sandía' (watermelon) and 'Agua de Tamarindo' (tamarind), both perfect for cooling down on a hot day while indulging in vibrant Mexican flavors.

Middle Eastern Delights

The Middle East offers a fragrant infusion of flavors. Pomegranate, revered in ancient times, is often juiced and enjoyed not just for its taste but also its myriad health benefits. Dates, another staple, are blended into creamy, sweet concoctions, often enjoyed during Ramadan to break the day-long fast.

Mango Mania in Southeast Asia

Southeast Asia, with its tropical climate, brings forth a bounty of fruits. Among them, mango stands out. In places like Thailand and the Philippines, mangoes are juiced, pulped, and even incorporated into smoothies with a touch of coconut milk, offering a sweet, creamy escape.

Conclusion

Reflecting on Your 30-Day Transformation

As the sun sets on your 30-day juicing odyssey, it's an opportune moment to pause and reflect on the profound metamorphosis you've undergone. When you embarked on this journey, you might have seen it as a simple, dietary change. But as the days progressed, it's clear that it was far more than just about what was in your glass. It became a transformative exploration of self-awareness, discipline, and a reconnection to nature's bounty.

The Ebb and Flow of Transformation

Change, as they say, is the only constant. And throughout these 30 days, change has been your loyal companion. There might have been days of exuberance when you felt invincible, riding the wave of energy that fresh, organic juices provided. But, perhaps there were also moments of challenge – days when temptation beckoned, or old habits clawed their way back. Yet, here you are, at the threshold of a month, having navigated the highs and lows with grace and determination.

Harvesting the Fruits of Your Labor

As you stand before the mirror, you might notice subtle shifts—a brighter glow in your complexion, that lightness in your step, or even a more restful slumber at night. These are the tangible benefits, the fruits of your labor. But look deeper, beyond the surface, and you'll find intangible changes too—a heightened clarity of thought, a deeper connection to your body's needs, and perhaps, a newfound appreciation for life's simple pleasures.

Carrying Forward the Lessons

The 30-day journey was not an end but a beautiful beginning. The lessons you've imbibed, the routines you've cultivated, and the flavors you've savored are treasures you'll carry forward.

As you transition into the tapestry of everyday life, remember to often revisit this transformative chapter. Use it as a touchstone, a reminder of your potential, resilience, and the radiant vitality that awaits when you honor your body and soul.

In this reflection, celebrate not just the transformation of your physique but the blossoming of your spirit. Here's to your journey, its challenges, its triumphs, and the many more adventures that lie ahead.

Embracing a Lifetime of Health and Vitality

Throughout this journey, you've unearthed the potent power of fresh produce, the magic of daily rituals, and the joy of mindful consumption. These discoveries aren't fleeting moments or temporary highs. They're timeless truths, pathways that lead to sustained well-being, and vitality that resonates from the inside out.

As the days transform into weeks and months, it's crucial to keep the flame of this newfound passion alive. Life, with its unpredictable twists and turns, will throw challenges, temptations, and distractions. But with the foundation you've built, and the knowledge you've gained, you are well-equipped to navigate them with grace, wisdom, and resilience.

The world of juicing and natural nutrition is vast, and every day presents an opportunity to learn, to experiment, and to deepen your understanding. Stay curious, remain open-minded, and let your passion for health be the compass that guides your choices and actions.

Remember, true vitality isn't just about the absence of illness. It's about the presence of zest, a vivacity that permeates every aspect of life. It's about waking up with a sparkle in your eyes, facing challenges with gusto, cherishing every moment, and retiring to bed with a heart full of gratitude.

Embracing a lifetime of health and vitality is not a task; it's a privilege. It's an invitation to dance with life, to savor its flavors, to cherish its moments, and to age with grace, strength, and poise. So, as you step forth into this new chapter, do so with confidence, love, and a spirit of adventure. Your journey has only just begun, and the best is yet to come.

Appendix

Glossary Of Terms

- **Cold Press**: A method of juicing that uses a hydraulic press to extract juice, preserving more nutrients and enzymes due to less heat and oxidation.
- **Enzymes**: Proteins that accelerate the rate of chemical reactions in the body. Sensitive to heat, they can be lost in some juicing processes.
- **Oxidation**: The process by which juice is exposed to oxygen, leading to nutrient degradation and a shorter shelf life.
- **Phytonutrients**: Natural compounds found in plants that provide health benefits. They often give fruits and vegetables their vibrant colors.
- **Pulp**: The solid remnants left after juicing a fruit or vegetable. Contains fiber and can be used in various recipes or composted.
- **Centrifugal Juicer**: Uses a fast-spinning metal blade to extract juice. Typically faster but can produce more heat, potentially reducing nutrient quality.
- **Masticating Juicer**: Machines that crush and press fruit and vegetables for the highest juice yield and nutrient retention. Also known as "slow" or "cold press" juicers.
- **Triturating Juicer**: Twin gear juicers that grind or rub the fruit and vegetable fibers together slowly to extract juice. Efficient with high nutrient retention.
- **Auger**: A tool in masticating juicers that crushes fruits and vegetables to release juice.
- **Chute**: The feeding tube of a juicer where produce is introduced for juicing.
- **Cruciferous Vegetables**: Includes broccoli, cauliflower, kale, and Brussels sprouts. Known for potential cancer-fighting properties.
- **Flavonoids**: Phytonutrients found in nearly all fruits and vegetables. Powerful antioxidants with anti-inflammatory and immune system benefits.
- **Terpenes**: Organic compounds responsible for aromatic oils in herbs and spices.
- **Organic Farming**: Agricultural method avoiding synthetic fertilizers and pesticides, emphasizing crop rotation, renewable resources, and soil conservation.
- **Synthetic Pesticides**: Chemicals used to prevent or repel pests. Residues can often be found on conventionally grown produce.
- **Balancing**: Ensuring optimal taste and nutritional value in a juice recipe.

- **Bioavailability**: Proportion of a nutrient having an active effect in the body. Enhanced by pairing specific ingredients.
- **Color Theory**: Creating visually appealing juices based on the harmony of colors and their impacts.
- **Curcumin**: Anti-inflammatory compound in turmeric known for its bright yellow color and health benefits.
- **Fat-soluble Vitamins**: Vitamins best absorbed when paired with dietary fats, including Vitamins A, D, E, and K.
- **Non-heme Iron**: Iron type primarily found in plant-based sources. Its absorption can be enhanced with vitamin C.
- **Nutrient Absorption**: Process by which the body absorbs and utilizes vitamins and minerals.
- **Piperine**: Alkaloid in black pepper enhancing the absorption of nutrients, especially curcumin from turmeric.
- **Synergy**: In juicing, the enhanced effect when ingredients are paired together, resulting in a greater combined effect.
- **Turmeric**: Golden-yellow spice known for its anti-inflammatory properties and its active compound, curcumin.
- **Vitamin C**: Necessary for growth and development. In juicing, enhances absorption of non-heme iron.

Additional Resources: Books, Blogs, and Communities

Books to Quench Your Thirst for Knowledge

1. ***"The Juicing Bible" by Pat Crocker***: This bestseller is not just a recipe book; it's a comprehensive guide that dives deep into the benefits of juicing, offering over 150 nutrient-rich recipes.
2. ***"Juice: Recipes for Juicing, Cleansing, and Living Well" by Carly de Castro, Hedi Gores, and Hayden Slater***: From the founders of the popular Pressed Juicery, this book provides insights into the art of juicing and its myriad health benefits.
3. ***"The Reboot with Joe Juice Diet" by Joe Cross***: This book chronicles Joe's journey of weight loss and health transformation using only natural juices, inspiring many to kickstart their own juicing adventure.

Blogs to Bookmark

1. ***Juice Guru***: This blog is a treasure trove of juicing tips, recipes, and techniques for both beginners and seasoned juicers.
2. ***The Rawtarian***: This space isn't just about juicing; it's a comprehensive guide to raw food living, but its juicing section is packed with invaluable insights.
3. ***Juicing with G***: This is where practical advice meets personal experience. From reviews on juicers to delicious recipes, this blog has it all.

Communities to Connect

1. ***r/Juicing on Reddit***: This community is bustling with juicing enthusiasts who share their recipes, success stories, challenges, and advice. It's an excellent platform for real-time interaction and guidance.
2. ***JuiceRecipes.com Forum***: An interactive platform where members share their favorite juice recipes, discuss the benefits of various ingredients, and provide support for those on juice fasts or cleanses.
3. ***Facebook Groups such as "Juicing for Health" and "Raw Juice Camp"***: These groups are filled with passionate individuals who offer advice, share their personal stories, and provide motivation for newcomers.

Measurement Conversion Table

Measurement (US)	Equals	Metric Equivalent
1/8 tsp	0.6 mL	
1/4 tsp	1.2 mL	
1/2 tsp	2.5 mL	
1 tsp	5 mL	
1 tbsp	15 mL	
1/4 cup	60 mL	
1/3 cup	80 mL	
1/2 cup	120 mL	
2/3 cup	160 mL	
3/4 cup	180 mL	
1 cup	240 mL	
2 cups (1 pint)	480 mL	
4 cups (1 quart)	0.95 L	
4 quarts (1 gallon)	3.8 L	

Measurement	Equals	Also Equals
1 tbsp	3 tsps	15 milliliters
1 cup	16 tbsps	237 milliliters

Measurement	Equals	Also Equals
1 ounce	1/16 pound	28.35 grams
1 pound	16 ounces	453.59 grams

Measurement Fahrenheit	Equals Celsius
225°F	110°C
250°F	130°C
275°F	140°C
300°F	150°C
325°F	165°C
350°F	180°C
375°F	190°C
400°F	200°C
425°F	220°C
450°F	230°C
475°F	245°C
500°F	260°C

Made in the USA
Middletown, DE
01 May 2024

53749078R00057